A GREENOCK MEMOIR

JANUARY 18, 2019
KINDLE DIRECT PUBLISHING

A Greenock Memoir
My early life and times spent in postwar Greenock

Jim Goodall

Including contributions from:

Iain Freer

Billy McFarlane

Matthew Stewart

Jack Glenny

Isobel Gray

Christine Paul

Rhianna Goodall

Justin Goodall

First Printing: 2012
This edition: 2018
ISBN: 9781790683314

Acknowledgements

Many people have helped me to write this book. Okay, they didn't stand over me with a whip, giving me a lash every time I made a spelling mistake or grammatical error, but without the following people, *A Greenock Memoir* might never have seen the light of day. Therefore, the following can take a figurative bow.

Firstly, thanks go to my family and friends, too many to mention, for the encouragement and recollections they provided me with when I decided to write this short memoir of my early life.

Their contribution included reminding me of some of the social and environmental events that took place in the 1940s, 1950s and 1960s about which I had forgotten.

Others who deserve a mention include Jack Glenny for giving me his kind permission to include his wonderful poem about recollections of Greenock past.

My appreciation also goes to Vincent Gillen of the McLean Museum, Greenock, for the encouragement he gave me a few years ago when he read the original manuscript, and for suggesting I should publish it in book form.

Finally, to Kathleen Bell for her dependable help and support, and who proofread every paragraph and suggested grammatical changes which greatly improved the finished composition of my storyline.

Oh! In addition, not forgetting you. Yes you, who hopefully will spend the time you will never ever see again reading the experiences I had when strolling down memory lane.

Any mistakes and memory lapses are my sole responsibility. However, in mitigation, I shall claim that all the events happened a long time ago. Therefore, I plead guilty to a wholehearted glow of fond memories.

Contents

1. Introduction

A few years ago, my granddaughter Rhianna Goodall asked me "what did you do in the War Granda?". I told her that in the middle of the War I burst into the World (and wondered how old did she think I was?). It turned out that she was working on a project at school about rationing during the War. I said that, although I was very young when the War ended, I could still remember many of the hardships that families endured. Therefore, I told her I would write down what I could remember about the consequences of rationing.

When I completed my little exercise, I realised that there was so much more I could have written about growing up in Greenock in the 1940s, 50s and 60s. Although at first glance this may appear to be a short time span, there were so many changes to our way of life that I thought I would put down in writing many of the adventures I, and many others of my generation, experienced along the way. What follows is the result of my efforts.

Before you start reading my story, please note that this is not a history of Greenock. Many people before me have already published excellent books about our little town, dating from the present time back to 1681 when the town became a free burgh of barony by charter granted by John Shaw.

Today (2018), we are now living in an age of uncertainty. The UK's vote on Brexit, the election of Donald Trump as President of the USA, the turmoil in many Middle East countries and the disruption in numerous European borders concerning their immigration policies. This is to name but a few. of the insecurities we face.

In addition to this, the speed of our lives, the pace of change and the introduction of new technologies can be quite bewildering to many of my generation. Therefore, I thought that now, being in the twilight years of my life, and so far just about managing to keep up with many of the high-tech wonders that embrace our lives, it would be the right time to do a bit of reverse time travelling and write my memoir of a childhood when I was raised in a simpler and slower-paced era. One, in which we were more intelligent than machines, rather than now when some machines seem to be more intelligent than us.

The recent Colour Report (2015) revealed that retirees rarely want to stop self-improving; with twelve per cent of us polled wishing to learn a new language or instrument, and a further twelve per cent of us would like to write a book during retirement. I am one of the latter, although recently, apart from this book, the most I have recently written is to sign my name on the latest doctor's prescription for pills and potions from the chemist that help keep my old limbs from slowly grinding to a halt.

The report also indicated that many elderly people think you're only as old as you feel, and there was also an overwhelming belief that they are not 'old', nor do they worry about getting old. In fact, 79% recently surveyed said they feel younger than their true age. I think that must be me they are writing about.

Evelyn Waugh, a renowned English author of novels, biographies and travel books, once wrote: "Only when one has lost all curiosity about the future has one reached the age to write an autobiography." I wonder what sad state of mind this celebrated writer was in when he expressed, in my humble opinion, such nonsense. I fully accept that what follows in this book is not strictly an autobiography, it's more snippets of recollections which cover a large slice of my early life from 1943 until 1964, but it most certainly does not mark a full stop to my inquisitiveness about what lies ahead of us. As Winston Churchill once wrote: "The farther backward you can look, the farther forward you are likely to see". How true.

So, before I start my story, let me introduce myself. My name is James Goodall, but I have always been known as Jim to my family and friends. I was born in the Rankin Memorial Hospital, Greenock, on Wednesday 3 February 1943, and was the first child of Albert and Mary Goodall (née Bolton). On Sunday 5 January 1947 my young brother Martin was born, also in the Rankin Memorial Hospital (which was later to have a major influence on both our young lives – see page 62 for further details).

Now that I have introduced myself, I want to move swiftly on to the main purpose of this little book. It was originally meant to inform my two sons, four grandchildren and anyone else who is interested, about the life and times I, and many of my peers lived through in Greenock in the 1940s, '50s and early '60s. And maybe, more importantly, to put my story down in writing while I can still sit back and summon snapshots frozen in time of a happy childhood before my memory retention starts to fade with age.

The following little tale is an example of why I decided to write about many of my experiences while I can still remember them.

As I made my way to the bar at a recent Burns Supper, a man about my own age, who was sitting at a table close by, shouted to me, "Jim, how are you doing? Long time no see." I walked over to him and we shook hands like old friends do, although to be honest, I had no idea who he was. My brain kicked into overdrive as I feverishly searched my internal databanks to see if I could remember something that would trigger my recognition buds, but nothing was forthcoming. Early pleasantries were soon dispensed with, and still I couldn't place where in my past this old "friend" had come from.

It should be appreciated that I had worked for 42 years at J.G. Kincaid, which was once a large local marine engineering company, and as I have many friends and work colleagues from the years I was there. Therefore, I assumed that the gentleman I was now deep in conversation with was from this era.

I appreciate that we all physically age over the years, especially men as they become more follically challenged, and what little hair is left often turns the colour of a snow-capped mountain as years' rush by. Even allowing for this, I still couldn't place the gentleman I was now conversing with. I'm sure most people of a certain mature age experience the same problem when someone, who at first glance means nothing to you, nods to you in the street or strikes up a conversation.

After about ten minutes of comparing notes which weren't falling into place, the mist lifted when he said, "It was great meeting you again, Jim", followed by the killer question as I turned to go back to the queue at the bar, "By the way Jim, are you still driving McGill's buses?" This stopped me dead in my tracks. I thought, "McGill's buses? What the hell is he talking about? I've never even been on one of their buses, never mind driving one!" He obviously saw the blank look on my face. "Are you not Jim McLeod from Port Glasgow?" he asked. "Not guilty," said I, "I'm Jim Goodall from Greenock.", "My God! You are his double" said my supposedly new friend. It was then that it suddenly dawned on us – we had been having a friendly ten-minute chat thinking we knew one another from our dim and distant past. We both burst out laughing at the ridiculous charade we had just acted out.

This is just one example of the effects of growing old, and when memories are no longer as clear as they once were. My mother always said, "The brain is like a box which can only take in so much information at a time. Therefore, if you insert something new, something old must be jettisoned from your grey matter to make way for it." I think she might have had a point there. So this is one of the reasons I have written this little memoir while I can still remember some of my past escapades.

However, I digress …

Donald Rumsfeld, former USA Secretary of Defense from 2001 to 2006 under President George W. Bush, once famously said, "because as we know, there are known knowns; there are things we know we know. We also know there are known unknowns; that is to say, we know there are some things we do not know. But there are also unknown unknowns -- the ones we don't know we don't know". Remember, this was from a man who once had his trigger finger on America's nuclear bomb button. I think we all dodged a very large bullet there!

When I started writing, I thought I would be lucky if I could fill half a dozen A4 pages covering the early period from my birth in 1943, until the birth of my younger son Allan in 1969.

How wrong I was, because as the project evolved, I found myself remembering more and more events which came flooding back to me through the mists of time. I soon found myself remembering friends and acquaintances I had a long time ago and wondering what had become of them, and whom amongst them had already shuffled off this mortal coil.

I also appreciated that, as both my parents, young brother, wife and many dear friends are now no longer with us, it meant that the world is no longer full of people whom I could share my memories with. Consequently, I did not want it to be just another memoir, as I thought no one would be interested in the mundane events of my early life. Before I started writing, I therefore took some time to consider how much detail I wanted to delve into. Did I really want to convey the routine activities together with the highlights? Would people be interested in the run-of-the-mill events I experienced growing up? Or would these just be quaint curiosities to them? A source I recently read recommended that "When writing a biography, cut back on the insights and beef up the anecdotes." Now that sounds like good advice to me.

After rummaging through these proposed principles, I realised that if I wanted to capture the spirit of the times, I had to be true to myself and tell my little narrative to the very best of my ability, and as well as my memory allowed. This meant that it will encompass as much detail as I could remember of growing up in Greenock in the 1940s, '50s and '60s. As I began writing I soon realised, moreover, that it was not just my story; it was in many ways the story of lots of others born into that era. Therefore, I decided that the aim of this project should also be to record my impressions of the environment in which I grew up in, and of some of the personal and social events which took place during that period.

It did not take me long to appreciate that the way of life I knew when I was a young boy had changed forever. And although there have been vast improvements in our general standard of living, sad to say, not all the changes have been for the better. Today, for example, many teenagers do not have a clue about how to wire a plug. Then again, dear reader, how often have you recently changed a plug? However, some of the same teenagers have the potential to hack into Fort Knox and bankrupt America with the click of a computer key. Is this progress? Yes, I suppose it is, but my, it is quite alarming!

It was also quite thought-provoking when I realised that the greatest part of my life is now confined to the history books, and that the clock is inexorably ticking away while there are still many things I want to say and do. In addition, since starting, to write this little Memoir, it has become obvious that, as the content evolved, it began to include areas which, hopefully, others may find of interest.

Unfortunately, my parents rarely spoke of their early lives growing up in their respective parts of Scotland (my mother was born and brought up in Greenock, and my father came from Cullen, Banffshire). Looking back on this now, I find the missing information a little bit disappointing, as I would have been interested to know what it was like for them in the 1920s and '30s.

Yes, my parents said life was tough and they did not have many of the material things I had when I was young (which were not many, I might add), but what was missing were many of the anecdotes and tales of the characters who must have been around in their youth. I wanted to ensure, therefore, that my little chronicle painted a verbal picture of what the world was like as I experienced it during the early stages of my life as a mid-20th-century boy.

In the current era, obviously, my two sons and four grandchildren are not fully aware of the kind of life I lived before they appeared on the scene. I remember thinking when I was young that, when I was older, and if I ever had any children, I would never repeat what many adults told me at the time (although not my Mum and Dad): "You don't realise how fortunate you kids are nowadays, son, because when we were young we never had so and so, and we had to do without this and that".

I certainly did not want to end up like some old codger sitting in a corner muttering away to myself about how tough it used to be in my time, and how kids today don't realise how lucky they are. I like to think that, for the most part, I have kept that promise I made to myself when I was young. That's one of the reasons why I would like to take this opportunity of acquainting my children, grandchildren and anyone else who might be interested, with a little of what the life and times were like as I, and many of my generation grew up in the latter half of the 20th century.

The following few paragraphs were plagiarised from the Internet, and I hereby hold my hands up and apologise to the unknown original author for using their text. Nevertheless, as it quite accurately describes much of what I also experienced when growing up, I thought I should share it here. Please note that I am not pontificating about our childhood being better than it is now. Indeed, in many ways, it is much safer today than it was back then, thanks to more health and safety restrictions. However, in some ways, the aficionados of political correctness have perhaps prevented today's children from experiencing much of the innocent fun we had in the 1940s, '50s and '60s. I quote the anonymous contributor.

"First, we survived being born to mothers who smoked and/or drank while they carried us (for the record, my mum did neither). They took aspirin, cooked with fat dripping and didn't get tested for diabetes. Then after that trauma, our baby cots were covered with bright coloured lead-based paints. We had no childproof lids on medicine bottles, doors or cabinets, and when we rode our bikes we had no helmets. As children, we would ride in cars without seatbelts or airbags. We drank water from the garden hosepipe and direct from the tap, NOT from a bottle (in many ways this was our contribution to the Green revolution we have today). We shared one soft drink bottle with our friends and no one actually died from this. Moreover, when the bottle was empty we took it back to the shop to get a few pennies back on the price. The shops then sent them back to the bottling plant to be washed, sterilized and refilled, so those same bottles were used over and over again, thus they really were recycled long before the term was used in everyday life. We ate cakes, white bread with real butter. And drank pop with sugar in it, but we weren't overweight because......
WE WERE ALWAYS OUTSIDE PLAYING GAMES!!

"We would leave home in the morning and play all day. Apart from coming back for our dinner (lunch to today's kids), we were out until the streetlights came on. No one was able to reach us all day. Moreover, we were OK. We would spend hours building our go-carts out of scraps and then ride down the hill, only to find out we forgot the brakes. After running into the bushes or a wall a few times, we learned how to solve the problem. We did not have PlayStations, Nintendos or X-boxes. There were no video games at all, no 99 channels on cable, no videotape movies, no surround sound, no mobile phones, no text messaging, no personal computers, no Internet or Internet chat rooms..........WE HAD FRIENDS and we went outside and found them! Imagination played a huge part in children's lives. We had one radio in the house that the family would gather round to listen to. Not a television the size of a tennis court in every room that splits the family up.

"We fell out of trees, got cut, broke bones and teeth and there were no lawsuits from these accidents. We played with worms (well some kids did – not me, I hasten to add). We made up games with sticks and tennis balls, and although we were told it would happen, we did not poke out any eyes. We rode bikes (without an inverted polystyrene fruit bowl on our heads) or walked to a friend's house and knocked on the door or rang the bell, or just yelled for them! Local teams had trials and not everyone made the team. Those who didn't had to learn to deal with disappointment. Imagine that! The idea of a parent bailing you out if we broke the law was unheard of. In many cases they actually sided with the law! Our generation produced some of the best risk-takers, problem-solvers, and inventors ever!

The past 60 years have seen an explosion of innovation and new ideas. We had freedom, failure, success and responsibility, and we learned how to deal with it all!"

Yes, our way of life then was very different from that of today's children, as we could play endlessly outside with little parental control. Few rules and regulations curtailed our carefree summer days. However, I am the first to admit that today's youngsters have such diverse experiences and commercial influences that we would love to have had back in the early postwar years.

The one new social innovation that tops many of the activities detailed above is, of course, the smartphone, which in some circumstances turns an ordinary member of the public into a paparazzi. Now, before I have my little grumble about them, I hereby state that I am certainly not a Luddite, as I freely admit that I have a smartphone, iPad and computer, and would hate to go back to the pre-mobile phone days.

However, it is disappointing now to see normal young, and sometimes not so young, people utterly oblivious to their surroundings and uninterested in what is happening around them, immersed in a world that is some distance from the one they are actually inhabiting. The signs are clear, the phones have started to rule our lives, rather than the other way around.

As smartphones are reportedly checked every 12 minutes (Ofcom 2018), it seems the only way to stop us using our devices is to take them away from us at certain times of the day. Not you and me of course, because we use ours responsibly. Of course we do. Don't we?

If you told some of today's children that there was once a world where smartphones did not exist, they would find it incomprehensible. As a teenager, when I wanted to meet up with friends at a future date, I had to make arrangements in advance while I was with them in the flesh, as few people had a land-line telephone, never mind a smartphone, in their house in those bygone days.

Nevertheless, I must be honest and admit that the smartphone's benefits far outweigh the downside of not making the effort to actually meet up with, and talk directly to, friends and family. However, one of the advantages of many typewriters made in the 1950s is that they still work today. Whereas smartphones, tablets and e-readers, with built-in obsolescence, are designed in such a way that they are ready for the black recycling bin after just a few years' usage.

The pictures opposite were of the mobile phone and email equivalents that were available when we were young, and indeed, in many areas, they are still in current use.

However, I must confess that I would be lost without the Internet and search engines like Bing, Yahoo and, of course, the behemoth that is Google. Then there are the social media

Figure 1 Our smartphone and email equivalents.

websites like Facebook, where many individuals regularly share their status and bare their souls before they even get out of bed in the morning. Today there are people who do everything online, for free: acquire music, download films, read a variety of documents and books, make friends and exchange information.

In addition to the above, we must not forget Internet banking, which allows us to check our account(s) in real time. However, it is sad to note that because of the changes in our banking habits, many of the major banks are closing down in numerous areas due to the infrequent use that is made of their facilities.

We also have the convenience of purchasing an item from the multitude of online shops there are and have it delivered to us on the same day. I have even self-published this book via an Internet publishing house, rather than trying to persuade literary agents that it is worthy of the Man Booker Prize for Literature and that they should go down on their bended knees and beg me to permit them the honour of publishing it.

At this rate, with many of us anchored to our chairs in front of a computer screen, in a few generations' time, our legs will have become redundant, as we conduct our daily lives from the comfort of an armchair in our own homes.

Yes, the World Wide Web is indeed a wonderful invention. It's just unfortunate that what many people do not do nowadays is clasp things in their hands. So when the Internet goes down or there is a power cut, there are no physical photographs to hold, no record collection to arrange. They all immediately disappear – the homework, the music, the photos and our friends.

However, this book is not about what we have today (2018), its main purpose is to reveal the cultural and physical differences between now and when I was young.

I have lost count of the number of times I thought I had finished recording my recollections, and then a new reminiscence would trigger some long-forgotten experiences or events that I had overlooked. Maybe a friend might say "remember so-and-so", and "ting!" a little bell goes off in the deep recesses of my brain and my laptop comes out to record this new information.

This, of course, results in more and more pages being added. The upshot is that this project looks as if it will be never-ending. Nonetheless, I have had to draw a line in the sand or I would never see the final printed article. Of course, this means that now, whenever I remember a subject I have previously missed, it will be too late to record it. Maybe a Volume Two of my little memoir will be the answer!

1943 events, in the year I was born:

Development of the Colossus computer by Britain to break German encryption codes during World War II.

Aqualung invented by, Jacques Cousteau and Emile Gagnan.

Great Depression ends in the United States: Unemployment figures fall fast due to World War II-related employment.

The Pentagon, considered to be the world's largest office building, is completed.

The Dambuster Raids on German dams by RAF 617 Squadron on 17th May on German dams.

In Iran, the Allied leaders of Britain, the United States and the Soviet Union meet for the first time.

The British and Americans bomb Hamburg, causing a firestorm that kills 42,000 German civilians.

Bengal, India, famine leaves up to three million dead.

1943 popular films:

For Whom the Bell Tolls – Gary Cooper and Ingrid Bergman

Lassie Come Home – Roddy McDowall and Donald Crisp

Edge of Darkness – Errol Flynn and Ann Sheridan

Song of Bernadette - Jennifer Jones and Charles Bickford.

Outlaw -Jane Russell, Thomas Mitchell and Walter Huston.

Stage Door Canteen - Benny Goodman and Count Basie.

1943 major world political leaders:

UK – Winston Churchill

USA – Franklin D. Roosevelt

Germany – Adolf Hitler

Japan – Hideki Tojo

Russia – Joseph Stalin

Italy – Benito Mussolini/Pietro Badoglio

1943 Historical prices, <u>not allowing</u> for inflation:

Commodity	1943 price	2013 price	% of male weekly wage	
			1943%	2013%
Petrol (gallon)	£0-2s 2d	£4.60	1.65%	1.13%
Pint of beer	£0-1s-2d	£2.40	0.98%	0.53%
Large loaf	£0-0s-9d	£1.50	0.65%	0.25%
Bottle whisky	£1-3s-0d	£14.00	19.00%	2.40%
Stamp	£0-0s-3d	£0.50	0.20%	0.10%

2013 Historical prices, <u>allowing</u> for inflation

Commodity	1943 price	2013 price	% of male weekly wage	
			1943%	2013%
Petrol (gallon)	£0-2s-2d	£8.91	3.60%	1.70%
Pint of beer	£0-1s-2d	£2.97	1.20%	0.57%
Large loaf	£0-0s-9d	£1.91	0.77%	0.37%
Bottle whisky	£1-3s-0d	£48.00	19.35%	9.25%
Stamp	£0-0s-3d	£0.42	0.17%	0.08%

1943 average weekly wage:

- Men: £6-1s-2d (£6.06)

  2013 equivalent amount allowing for inflation – £248

  2013 average weekly earnings for full-time employees - £517

- Women: £3-11s-0d (£3.55)

  2013 equivalent amount allowing for inflation – £142

  2013 Women's earnings are 10% lower than men's.

A sum of £3-12s-6d was normally written as £3-12-6, but a sum of 12s 6d was normally recorded as 12/6.

When I was born in 1943, the money then in circulation was:

Farthing (abolished 1961).
Halfpenny (colloquially known as ha'penny and abolished 1969).
Penny and thruppenny bit (three pence) (demonetised 1971).
Sixpence (demonetised 1980).
One shilling.
Florin (two shillings, demonetised 1993).
Half-crown (two shillings and sixpence, demonetised 1970).
Ten-shilling note (demonetised 1971).
Pound note (demonetised, England, 1988)
Five-pound note.
Higher denominations were available, but were usually out of reach of working-class families.

Figure 2 1971 pre-decimal coins

The following table compares pre-decimal currency to decimal currency.

Pre-decimal currency	Equivalent to	Decimal equiv.
Two farthings	One halfpenny	N/A
Two halfpence	One penny (1d)	0.42 pence
Three pence	One thruppence (3d)	1.25 pence
Six pence	One sixpence, "tanner"	2.50 pence
Twelve pence	One shilling, "bob" (1s)	5.00 pence
Two shillings	One florin, "two-bob bit"	10.00 pence
Two shillings & six pence	One half-crown	12.50 pence
Five shillings	One crown	25.00 pence

Since I was born, the world has seen more changes than in any other period of human history. The coming of the digital age has revolutionised the access we have to the media. This means that we have instant interaction with news, music, videos, communication and all the other kinds of wondrous things that were undreamt of when I was a child.

I feel very privileged to have lived through this upsurge of wonderful new technology and confess that I am unashamedly a "gadget man" who embraces all this new knowledge with great enthusiasm, even though I often look back to when I was a young boy and think of the innocent pleasures we had then.

We could never have imagined that the onset of new technology in the late 20th century would produce items like personal computers and smartphones (that I have dealt with earlier) which, in addition to their main communication functions, can take high-quality pictures and videos. They can even link us via satellites to the other side of the world in an instant. It must be appreciated that we hadn't even heard of satellites until history was made on 4 October 1957, with the Soviet Union's successful launch of Sputnik I, the world's first artificial satellite. After many years, satellite technology eventually enabled us to access satellite-based global positioning systems which allow us to drive to our chosen location with the minimum of fuss.

To put my early-life biography into perspective, when I was eight years old King George VI was our Monarch and Winston Churchill was the Prime Minister. I had never seen a television set or been in a private motor car. I hadn't heard of or eaten a burger. Chinese, Indian and other ethnic food restaurants were totally alien to us. Rock 'n' Roll music was still unheard of, supermarkets were only starting to arrive in the high street, and the Internet was almost fifty years away in the future.

Do I like being a Senior Citizen? In many ways, yes I do. After all, inside most older people is a younger person wondering what the hell happened to them along the way.

Please appreciate that I have tried to write this short story without the aid of rose-tinted glasses, although no doubt the warm glow of a happy childhood often seeps through. Therefore, I hereby plead guilty to a large dose of gentle nostalgia, as it is a wonderful part of the human experience for those of us of a certain age.

Recently researchers at Warwick University concluded that 1957 was the best year in Britain's history. It seems they had researched eight million books published between 1776 and 2009, and they claimed that all the evidence suggested that in 1957 – with postwar rationing over (except for coal rationing, which ended in June 1958), full employment and the great engine of consumerism now in full flow – life was getting better for a large majority of people.

Being only fourteen at the time, I obviously can't remember how accurate this information is, but I certainly can't make a case against it.

Please don't let me give the impression that I'm against the march of progress and have a grievance against the modern world. Not so. I just don't like the past being dismissed out of hand. Not everything is bunkum just because it's older, including me.

Before you carry on reading my story, please note that I have never written a book before, and you have probably never written one either; so there we have it – a friendly connection has been established between writer and reader. And as tempting as it was to embellish a few particularly uncomfortable moments in my life, I decided that however unpalatable the truth was, I would stick to it no matter what.

Consequently, if you can remember the likes of early TV programmes such as Dixon of Dock Green, Z Cars, Crackerjack, Bill and Ben the Flowerpot Men and Juke Box Jury, then this book will be for you. If they mean absolutely nothing to you, then hopefully you will still find it interesting to see how we old codgers survived without the multitude of programmes that proliferate our television sets today.

Regrettably, as the years' advance, and we get older, the sun stops ambling across the sky and starts moving as if someone had hit the fast-forward button. Yes, while Old Father Time marches on, blink and you can almost miss a month.

I hope therefore that the biographical reminiscences, information and anecdotes of social history which follow, many of them light-hearted, combined with personal milestones, are of interest and will hopefully give insights into the general changes in society, intermingled with the different phases of my life from my early childhood through to my early twenties.

I fully appreciate that my narratives are a little inclined towards a boy's and young man's perspective of the postwar era. However, I hope both sexes can relate to many of the milestones we shared in the years I have written about.

As Michael Parkinson, journalist and broadcaster, once said, "Memory Lane is a great place to go. You always seem to meet a better class of people down Memory Lane." How true.

So sit down and make yourself comfortable while I take you on the journey that was my life in the 1940s, '50s and early '60s. It took me approximately 25 years going the long way. You should manage it in a couple of hours.

2. Wartime memories

You will note from my earlier introduction that I was born during World War Two, the Second World War, WWII or whatsoever else you might like to call it. However, we grew up calling it "the War". Older readers must remember the war: I'm sure it was in all the papers. I was about 30 months old when the fighting ended. This, of course, meant that I was too young to remember the hostilities very much as it raged throughout Europe and the Far East.

While all around there was also a huge sense of relief when the War ended with the surrender of Germany and Italy in May 1945, followed by Japan in September of the same year. At my tender age, I did not appreciate the hardships that were endured by the populace at the time. During this period, it should be noted, the after-effects of the War were constant topics of conversation e.g.: food, clothes, entertainment, separation, loss, rationing, reunion and so on.

However, wartime values and standards were still very strong. Respectability, conformity and restraint were what underpinned most of the 1940s and '50s. Yet it would be wrong to assume that Britain in this era was a land of carefully calibrated politeness, although this image was helped by public spaces being informally policed by the likes of bus conductors and park-keepers, and by a resolute police force that was largely admired. This was, for the many, an age of trust.

As the War was still very fresh in everyone's mind, young boys like us loved to mimic our movie star favourites, re-enacting War games with the brave British "Tommies" shooting the horrible "Jerries" with our toy guns when playing outside. Never in my wildest dreams could I have imagined that children (and many adults too) would still be playing war games sixty years later, albeit on their game consoles and computers.

Although the conflict had finished about a year and a half earlier, when I was four years old I became a War casualty by proxy. My War wound, which I was very proud of at the time, came about when I was watching a barrage balloon drifting in the sky above me. For those of you who are unfamiliar with what a barrage

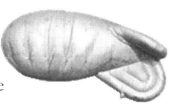

Figure 3 Barrage Balloon

balloon was, it was a large dirigible, sometimes called a "blimp", which was tethered to the ground with metal cables. The top of the balloon was filled with hydrogen and the bottom half was left empty.

The balloon would be raised or lowered to the desired altitude by a winch. When it was hoisted to the recommended height, it then filled with natural air which made it expand to its designed dimensions. Its purpose was to help defend the people on the ground against an air attack from enemy planes by damaging or destroying the aircraft if it collided with the cables, or at the very least making the attackers' approach much more hazardous.

How did my war wound come about? Well, one afternoon there was great excitement throughout our area when it was noted that a large balloon had somehow broken free from its moorings and was floating across the sky above our heads. I have no idea why this balloon had still been secured to the ground, as the War had been over for a couple of years. Nonetheless, it had somehow managed to free itself from its anchorage and had started to disappear over one of the high tenement buildings. To get a better view, I stepped backwards and went head over heels over a fence-post that had been hammered into the ground. As I was falling, I put my hand down on the ground to try and save myself but, when I landed, there was a loud crack and my left arm broke just above the wrist.

There was none of the British stiff upper lip from me. Oh no, I cried my eyes out with the pain as I was rushed to the Greenock Royal Infirmary, which was then situated at the bottom of Duncan Street (where John Galt House is now). Fortunately, this was only about half a mile from our old tenement flat at the corner of Sir Michael Street and Roxburgh Street. The bone was soon reset, and a plaster cast fitted by the hospital staff. It should be noted that this happened just before the National Health Service came into existence (that did not come into effect until 5 July 1948).

To help ease the pain and keep my spirits up, I was told that I was now a War hero as I had been injured in action trying to prevent the barrage balloon floating away. This made me feel much better. However, I kept wondering why my Victoria Cross medal never arrived (I was constantly told that it was in the post).

Another consequence of the War ending was the many War films that hit the silver screens in the late 1940s and early '50s, while the experience was still fresh in everyone's mind. This certainly helped to sustain the ailing British film industry at the time. Their War movies contained representations of real events with real people, and when I was growing up they were one of the mainstays of popular film culture. Although I was only about fourteen years of age when I first saw it, my favourite war film then, and now, was *The Cruel Sea*, with the inimitable Jack Hawkins, whose towering performance exuded natural dignity, despair and effortless authority in the crucial central role.

This film, to me, was a cut above the rest for its realism as there were no striking heroic deeds in the story. Instead, it detailed real people doing onerous and often dangerous jobs to the very best of their ability. This film certainly conveyed to the audience the horrors of naval warfare.

Other popular British War films that are still shown on television today and evoke the courage, heroism, patriotism and common decency of those they portrayed, included *The Dam Busters, The Malta Story, Sink the Bismarck, Ice Cold in Alex, Battle of the River Plate, Reach for the Sky* and *The Colditz Story*, to name but a few.

One thing nearly all these films had in common was the good old British class system. Almost all the officers were Oxbridge-educated middle-class types, whilst the other ranks consisted of stereotypical cheeky Cockneys, dour Scots engineers, Welsh singers and Yorkshire "Tykes", with Birmingham Brummies and Liverpool Scousers making up the rest of the cast.

Figure 4 Popular British War Films

However, we mustn't forget how film stars such as John Wayne, Audie Murphy and other erstwhile American "heroes" won the War single-handed for us poor old Brits (according to Hollywood, that is), although I am being very unkind to Mr Murphy who was, in reality, a highly decorated War hero.

Whereas Mr Wayne never enlisted, even though he was reported to be eligible to do so.

Many legends and myths were told of the local men who served their country with bravery and distinction. A fine example I recently heard about was the following little story, which I think is a little apocryphal, is about a doughty lady and her husband who lived in a Greenock "single end" tenement flat along with their two young children. For the sake of the story, we will call them Ann and John. However, I'll not divulge their surname; mainly to protect John, who fought abroad in mainland Europe, serving King and country.

This epic tale starts in Crete during WWII when John's platoon lost many of their men during a German assault on their position. Following the brutal firefight, there were only about a dozen men left to defend their area. John, who was a Corporal in his regiment, found himself to be the most senior survivor left alive. This, of course, meant he had to take all the command decisions. During a short lull in the battle, John bravely crawled up a small mound to get a better view of the enemy and saw that there were over a hundred German troops surging up a hill towards them. Being a strong-willed man brought up in the rough-and-tumble of the back streets of Greenock, and using his experience fighting the Germans in North Africa and Italy, he decided to make the only decision possible under the circumstances - he surrendered.

Following their capture, John and his men were transferred to a prisoner-of-war camp in Czechoslovakia. After a few months there, he was allowed to write a short message on a postcard to his wife in Greenock, as up until then she had only been told that John was "missing in action". He wrote and said that life was very tough being a prisoner in the Stalag prison camp, as the living conditions were appalling He also advised her that he was very depressed but would struggle on regardless.

Many weeks later, he received a letter back from Ann. We now get to the crux of the story. Fully expecting Ann to send him words of comfort and support, he was shocked to read: "What do you mean you find it xxxxxx tough there? What about me trying to bring up two weans alone in a xxxxxx Greenock single end flat on a measly War pension? Get a xxxxx grip man and consider yourself lucky." You will appreciate that I have deleted all the expletives from her reply to protect the innocent amongst you.

When the War was finally over, and John was about to be repatriated back home, he realised that he had a very hard choice to make. Should he return to face the wrath of the feisty Ann, or maybe take the easier option of becoming a bull elephant sperm collector? Now that was a difficult decision he had to make.

The moral of the story is, "Don't expect sympathy from a Greenock housewife living in a run-down small tenement flat with two kids to bring up on her own, even if you were a dinner, bed and breakfast guest of Herr Hitler for a few years".

This was just one of the multitude of stories that did the rounds. Paradoxically, many men rarely mentioned the sights and sounds they experienced during this traumatic period in our history.

When the War finally ended, most of the service personnel went back to peacetime employment. However, to ensure we would still have a military presence in the world, National Service was introduced in 1947 to replace wartime conscription. It began properly at the beginning of 1949, and would last until 1963, bringing more than two million young British men into the armed forces.

From 1 January 1949, healthy 17 to 21-year-old males were required to serve in the armed forces for 18 months, and then remain on the reserve list for a further four years. In October 1950, in response to the British involvement in the Korean War, the service period was extended to two years; in compensation, this period was reduced by six months. I was fortunate, or unfortunate depending on your point of view, to miss my "call-up" by about 18 months when I was 17.

We are informed today (2013 when I was writing this particular paragraph) that we live in an age of austerity due to the financial crisis of 2007-2008. However, this is nothing compared to the self-denial that was endured after World War II. Rationing was still in force, and people had to count every penny (more of this later).

Indeed, the consequences of the disastrous aftermath of World War II, which had been over for quite a few years, could still be seen all around us. Looking back now, I well remember a monochrome world of blackened exterior walls, outside toilets and the dread of lung diseases such as tuberculosis and chronic bronchitis.

Yes, Britain was a nation exhausted by War. Although victorious, it had drained the country of men, money and resources. Thankfully, these days are long gone, and we have now metamorphosed into a much brighter place. Then again, when I look at the depressing daily news from around the world, I sometimes wonder if we really have.

Figure 5
Wartime Ration Book

However, we have now entered a new technological age that will ultimately change the way we live, work and interact with each other. Hopefully, this new digital age will transform lives and will bring many benefits to us all.

Another of the War's legacy that affected everyone throughout, and a few years after the hostilities, was food and fuel rationing. It began in September 1939 when the first commodity to be controlled was petrol. On 8 January 1940 bacon, butter and sugar were rationed. This was followed by successive ration schemes for meat, tea, jam, biscuits, breakfast cereals, cheese, eggs, lard, milk, and canned and dried fruit.

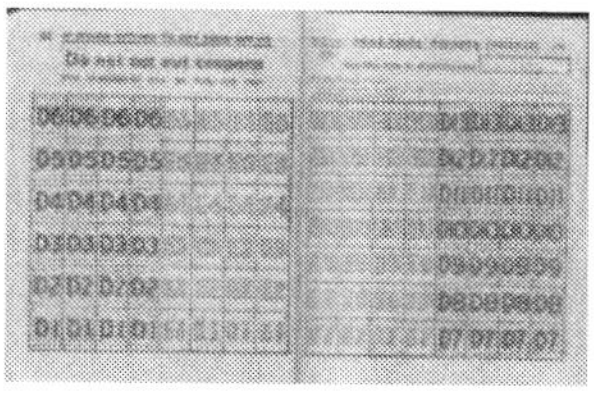

Figure 6 Wartime Ration Book

In order for the 21st-century generation who may have been coerced into reading this little journal to appreciate the hardship that families had to endure, I thought it might be appropriate to detail some of the items which could only be purchased with money plus ration book stamps. For the assistance of the readers among you who were born after the monetary decimalisation took place, I've taken the liberty of converting the currency from pounds, shillings and pence into decimals, and the weight from ounces to grams (gm).

- **Bacon and ham**: 2 oz (56 gm) per person a fortnight
- **Cheese**: ½ oz (14 gm) a week
- **Butter/margarine**: 7 oz (200 gm) a week
- **Cooking fats**: 2 oz (56 gm) a week
- **Meat**: One shilling's (5 pence) worth a week
- **Sugar**: 8oz (225 gm) a week
- **Tea**: 2oz (56 gm) a week
- **Chocolates and sweets**: 4 oz (110 gm) a week
- **Eggs**: No fixed ration: 1 egg for each ration book when available
- **Milk**: 3 pints a week
- **Preserves**: 4 oz (110 gm) a week

Bread, soap, bananas and potatoes were also rationed during this period. In 1951, families could buy only 10d (4 pence) worth of meat each week. Two more commodities were rationed after the War. Bread was rationed from 1946 to 1948 and potatoes for a year from 1947. Although this was a challenging way of life, at least it guaranteed a nutritious if dull diet.

The points system came to an end in 1950, but rationing continued until 1954 when meat was finally taken off the ration books.

During this particular period, an illegal black market flourished. This was when many otherwise honest people contributed to a subversive economy, sourcing many of the aforesaid items on the black market and paying over the odds for them without needing ration books.

An example of rationing that affected us kids was the sweet rationing. I still remember the time (I was then about five or six years old) when a rumour went around the streets like wildfire indicating that a small sweet shop in the West Station area was selling tablet (the sugary kind which almost makes your teeth rot as you eat it, not the synthetic Apple iPad kind you get today). Off I went to find my Mum as fast as my little legs would carry me, to beg for the 3d (1p), and, more importantly, the ration coupon which would allow me to buy this precious treat.

On receiving the coupon and money I ran to the shop, only to find a queue of my peers who had the same aim as me: to buy the rarely seen lesser-spotted tablet bar. Taking my turn at the back of the queue, I prayed there would still be enough tablet left for me by the time I got to the front. Finally, I reached the counter and, joy of joys, I managed to purchase the craved-for sweet delight.

I use this tablet story as a metaphor for how excited we were when the longed-for treat or special occasion became a reality. Youngsters throughout the years have always felt the same level of expectation and exhilaration when this happens to them. It's only the magnitude or value of the desired item that's changed, e.g. when I was young I always wanted a cowboy's toy gun that could fire "caps" (a cap gun is a toy gun that creates a loud bang, along with a puff of smoke, that

Figure 6 Toy pistol with caps

is meant to simulate a gunshot when a small percussion cap,

approximately 1.4 to 1.8 millimetres in diameter, is hit when the gun's trigger is fired), whereas today's youngster dreams of an iPad, game station or similar luxury electronic gadget.

As a young lad in the 1940s and '50s, I did not really appreciate the adversity many suffered since this was the only way of life I had ever known. However, please do not think that when I was a child I lived in a state of deprivation and poverty. Far from it, for my abiding memory is of a happy and secure childhood, free from many of the social problems that now afflict modern society.

As detailed in my introduction earlier in the book, we would always play games outside with our friends in a relatively safe neighbourhood environment that we took for granted, especially as there was hardly any road traffic about.

Adults did not seem to panic. Nothing seemed to stop them letting us go out to play. They seemed to understand the intrinsic need for children to take risks and learn the basic life lesson that actions have consequences. At the age of four or five (no pre-primary playschools then), our parents encouraged, and in many cases ordered, us to play outside so that we would "not get under their feet". We would cross our reasonably quiet suburban roads to play with other children all morning. This only ended when our mothers summoned us home for our midday dinner. These were cooked, as a rule, to a tight budget, and were normally taken together as a family. It should be noted that back then the midday meal was "dinner", not lunch, and our evening meal was "tea-time", not dinner. We had two choices: when it came to the food that was put down before us: "take it" or "leave it".

We usually gulped down our meals as quickly as possible, so we could get back outside and resume whatever game we were playing. We romped and explored the surrounding environment from a safe base, such as barren wasteland and derelict buildings – all the delicious fraught things that attract young boys. Yes, we all had the wonderful "Restless Legs Syndrome".

When we were a bit older, we played games such as marbles, French cricket, rounders, tig ("you're het" was the call when you were caught), hide-and-go-seek and kick the can. Rather than try to explain the rules of these games, I would suggest that you explore the internet's search engines for an explanation.

However, football was the game of choice for many of the boys in our area, as all that was needed was a ball, a piece of waste ground or an empty street, and a few sweaters or jackets for goalposts.

The imaginary crossbar was always a source of controversy, as the height of it from the ground was usually determined by how tall the goalkeeper was at the time.

Figure 7 Street football in the 1950s

Teams were selected when the two boys, who were universally accepted as the best players, picked alternate boys for their team. The last two left standing were usually a few years younger and smaller than the rest and had to accept that they were cannon fodder. Because of this, they normally ended up being the goalkeeper. It should be noted that there was rarely such thing as eleven-a-side then. It just depended on how many turned up. This meant the game could be anything between five to a fifteen-a-side. Of course, this meant that you could be playing for ten minutes before you even got a kick of the ball.

As we grew older, we dreamed of playing for Scotland one day. When we realised we were not quite good enough for that career move, we would downgrade our dream to one of playing for the mighty Greenock Morton. However, if we were honest, we were more than happy just playing with our pals on some deserted piece of waste ground.

In our group of boys, a couple of them were highly skilled players, indeed, they turned professional in their late teens and joined senior football clubs. The rest of us were pretty average, but at the end of the day it didn't really matter, as we were pals who enjoyed each other's company playing the "beautiful game". Mind you, in my head I was brilliant; I had a great footballing brain. I had a terrific shot. I could see the pass and make a fabulous tackle. Unfortunately, there was a wire missing between my brain and my feet, and this wire was a very important one, as it should have dispatched the information from my head to my toes in double quick time, but invariably failed to do so, and therefore the moment was lost.

For many girls, it was skipping ropes and hopscotch/peever (the rules, to this day, I have never understood). This was an era when girls played outside with girls and boys played with other boys.

When not playing football or riding our bikes, we discussed masculine things, like who was the person to avoid at marbles or conkers, or who had the best comics to swap? Yes, our social activities knew no boundaries. In addition, although we had far fewer material things than children have today, I think there was more togetherness and camaraderie because we had to make our own outdoor entertainment. In doing so, we made many more friends instead of being stuck in the house watching television or playing games on a computer or tablet.

Instead of the Internet, we had libraries. Instead of 24-hour television, there were the anarchic Saturday matinée picture shows. Moreover, when we were young teenagers, instead of playing with iPads and smartphones, we huddled under the bedclothes at night to listen to pop music on Radio Luxembourg.

I suspect we were far more creative than kids sitting in front of their computers today are. What lucky children we were! Being able to make things gave us great confidence and self-assurance. All sorts of natural and man-made objects were grist to our mill. Unfortunately, in many ways, manual inventiveness has gone out of the window in this age of computers, although I would be the first to admit that it is great to see young children embracing new technology. It's just a pity that most of that happens alone, in the confines of their rooms.

Life today, and since the '50s and early '60s too, has changed dramatically since my infancy. Imagine a country where countless doors were left unlocked, and with people really looking out for each other. Kids played in the communal back greens and in the streets, as there was little traffic about. We were safe. Indeed, we had almost as much chance of being knocked down by a horse and cart as by a car or lorry.

We climbed trees, skinned our knees, ripped our clothes, got into fights, and nobody sued anyone else at the drop of an ambulance-chasing lawyer's hat. Fantasy? No, just some of the enjoyable times we had in Greenock back in the 1940s and '50s of my youth.

A big plus for us kids in the 1940s and 50s was that, compared with today, there was fewer traffic on the roads. In 1955 there were just over three million licenced cars on U.K. roads. Contrast that with the 2014 total of over 31 million cars on the highways today. Of course, this meant it was much safer then to play outside without the fear of heavy traffic roaring along the roads.

Figure 7 1955
Road Tax Disk

The picture opposite is of an old Tax Disk that had to be displayed on every car's windscreens at all times.

Almost from our first day at school in Primary 1, we walked to and from school alone or with our friends. It was extremely rare for parents to take their children to school or collect them when school finished. Sweets were a treat for us, not part of lunch. Sherbet dabs, Jubbly drinks, dolly mixtures, sugarally straps, gobstoppers and homemade tablet were just some of the sugary items we devoured at a rate of knots when available. This obviously contributed greatly to widespread tooth decay which often meant a dreaded visit to the school dentist, which to us was the equivalent of the Spanish Inquisition's torture chamber.

As kids, we had a mixture of fear and respect for figures of authority such as parents, teachers, the police "bobby", doctors and park keepers. I appreciate this was in part generated by some slight physical and verbal abuse, but it worked. Older people were called "Mr" and "Mrs". And we normally only spoke to them when spoken to.

Figure 8 . A 'Bobby' on his Beat

Many boys of my generation had what was then considered sensible names like James, Robert, William, Patrick, Paul and John (for 2015 it was: Jack, Oliver and James). I was pleased to note that my First name has stood the test of time. The top three names for girls were Mary, Barbara and Patricia (for 2015 it was: Emily, Sophie and Olivia).

I well remember an amusing tale told by comedian Billy Connelly. He said that when he was a boy he had a friend that had a nickname called "Genghis". When he was asked why he called him that, he said his pal's surname was "McCann".

3. Old Britain

The 1950s marked the last decade of "old Britain" because, for countless prior generations, this was a period when many men and women were not treated as equals both at home and at work. The general convention then was that the majority of women did not have real careers. Instead, they were expected to look for short-term employment before they got married, and then to stop work after they had children. Once their children had arrived, they were expected to stay at home, take care of the children, and to cook, clean and keep the home neat and tidy.

Thankfully, women today play a much greater role in society than they had in the 1950s and countless years before this. Many now have a salaried work career in addition to tending to household chores. They also contribute to the family budget working at jobs, that in my childhood days, would have been unheard off.

As for the men, they were regarded as the main breadwinners of the family, and were expected to go out and work to earn enough money to keep the wolf from the door. They were also expected to discipline the children and be the head of the house. Fortunately, many men today now accept equal responsibilities with their wives and partners and do their fair share of the household duties.

When I was a young lad the vast majority of men wore headgear of varying design. This often denoted their social standing in the community. Flat caps were considered appropriate for manual workers, while middle-class white-collar working men usually donned a suit with a shirt and necktie, topped off with a soft hat.

Fortunately, the wearing of a hat and cap lost its obligatory status symbol over the years. However, the necktie most certainly did not. This was also considered a badge of honour on working days for some men, as many considered that it indicated that they worked in an office rather than being tagged as a shop floor or manual worker. It should be noted that this mandatory tradition is slowly dying out.

As for young boys like myself in the 1950s, we were expected to wear short knee-length trousers and caps to primary school.

Were they really the good old days for us kids? Perhaps, because, in our nostalgic view of the past, we are tempted to think that it was so much safer and more innocent. In many ways it was, but there were plenty of failings and weaknesses similar to what we experience today.

Unfortunately, we never had any great aspirations to improve our lifestyle. This was in part because we did not really know that there was a better life we could aspire to just waiting out in the big-wide-world.

Looking back to our early childhood, we imagine that in the summertime the sun always shone through a cloudless sky, and in the winter months' perfect crisp snow would fall and cover the ground with a textbook white blanket so that we could play with our sledges for days on end. Of course, this was not the case, but what is the harm in enjoying the memory?

I sometimes wonder if the warnings about global warming are coming true quicker than we are informed, as we seemed to have had many more snowfalls back in the 1940s and '50s than we have today (although the Beast from the East in early 2018 was an exception to the earlier presumption).

One such winter was in 1947 when from 22 January to 17 March, snow fell every day somewhere in the UK! The temperatures very rarely rose more than a degree or two above zero. A personal example of the effects of this blast of icy weather from the Arctic wastes was that after my young brother Martin came into the world on 5 January 1947, the severe weather meant he hardly ever left the house from the middle of January until late March.

The UK's population, which totalled about 50 million in 1950, was overwhelmingly indigenous. The 1951 census showed that only three per cent of the population had been born overseas, and the great majority of these immigrants were white Europeans. In 1950 it was estimated there were no more than 20,000 (0.004%) residents of other races in Britain, almost all of them born overseas.

Even though I was born a couple of years before what is euphemistically called the Baby Boomer years (usually referring to those born between, and including, 1946 and 1964), my generation is often included in this demographic period. It is sad to note that many supposedly contemporary commentators berate this age group now as property-hogging and economically privileged. We are supposed to have placed an "unsustainable burden on taxpayers". Indeed, our contemporary Jeremy Paxman, broadcaster, journalist and author, once wrote: "It's a wonder that young people aren't out on the streets demanding compulsory euthanasia for the Baby-Boomers". Moreover, he did not have his tongue in his cheek when he wrote it.

What he, and the other critics, should remember is that many Baby Boomers of today contributed a similar percentage of their salary to their parents' pension comparable, allowing for inflation, as to what today's working generation are now contributing. Yes, it may have been a much smaller amount in actual currency, but in real terms, the impact on the working person's take-home wage was quite similar to the effect it has on today's workforce.

I would simply ask the detractors to note that when I was a five-year-old Baby Boomer I was very grateful to receive a little cake, an orange and a small tin soldier for my Christmas. If a young child was offered that today, they would look upon it as a punishment for some horrendous wrongdoing they had committed.

Another plus for the Baby Boomer generation is that in many ways we were the first "Green Generation", although we did not realise that at the time. We returned various types of glass bottles (mainly lemonade ones)to the shops in order to collect a small deposit paid on them. The shops then sent them back to the bottling plant to be washed, sterilised and refilled, resulting in those bottles being constantly recycled. Today (2018) the vast majority of bottles are made of plastic and are polluting our environment when, instead of being recycled properly, they are abandoned on our streets, parks and beaches. However, it is pleasing to note that many major drinks brands are now open to the idea of a deposit-return scheme (DRS) like the one we had when I was a child, although I wouldn't hold my breath for any length of time waiting for this to come into general practice.

Other savings that were made was when babies' nappies were washed, dried and reused, instead of thrown away like the disposable ones we have now. Another "Green" practice was that clothes which had been washed were dried on an outside, weather permitting, rope line, not in an energy-gobbling tumble dryer burning up 220 volts at a fast rate of knots. Wind and solar power really did dry our clothes back in the Baby Boomer days.

Please note that I am not criticising all the improvements in health, science, technology and the general quality of life we have today. No, all I am trying to do is to bring our frugal, environmentally friendly practices we had then, to the attention of those who complain that our generation was responsible for many of the problems we have now. Indeed, the opposite is true, as we contributed to many of the advances detailed above.

Moreover, most senior citizens do not like being old in the first place. And it doesn't take much to really annoy us, especially from so-called academics who spout nonsensical views that they will almost certainly change when they reach our age. They should also appreciate that when today's Baby

Boomers walk into a room and remember why they went in there in the first place, it is quite an achievement. And another thing, don't forget that when we talk to ourselves, we are asking for expert advice!

There are some other things that let you know you're getting older too, but I can't remember what they are…Oh, yes, memory. Luckily, at the moment my memory only plays tricks on me, like when I try to remember the name of a film star I saw on a movie the previous evening, yet I can still clearly remember many things that happened 65 years ago.

I could go on with this little rant, but I think I'd better stop now as hopefully, I've made my point. After all, I don't want to be tarred with the brush of being a grumpy old man (which I like to think I'm certainly not).

I will also take this opportunity to advise that education about the dangerous use of drugs and related illegal substances was unheard of when I was a youth at secondary school. The reason for this was simple; it was because drugs were almost unknown in our community. Recreational stimulation for us was riding our bikes, kicking a football about and generally playing outside with our friends. Was life more innocent before the Internet? I like to think it was.

Sure, we said things when we were young that certainly would not be considered politically correct in today's world, some of which I freely admit I would cringe at if I travelled back in time and listened to myself. However, it was never meant to be particularly malicious, it was just a sign of the times, unfortunately. Regrettably, it is a sad fact of life that in the 21st century some people cross the red line of good taste on social media websites every day. Especially when invited to bare their souls in public, they take great delight in doing so in an offensive manner. Yes, some people should be rated at 9.9 out of 10 in a "Don't-Give-a-Toss-Meter".

It has recently been reported (1 December 2012) that the number of children taken to hospital A & E departments after being hurt at home has soared over the past decade, while the number injured playing outdoor sports, tumbling off skateboards, falling from trees etc. has fallen considerably.

It should be noted that we walked or rode our bikes to school instead of turning our parents into a 24-hour taxi service in the family's car or van, which now cost about what a new four-bedroom detached house did then.

It has also been recently reported (2016) that Scotland's children are among the least active in the world, in spite of our country having one of the best environments for outdoor play and sports. A study of 38 countries by the University of Strathclyde put Scotland joint bottom for physical activity and the overuse of computer screens.

Unfortunately, these figures paint a depressing picture of today's children turning their backs on the traditional outdoor adventures in favour of getting their thrills in front of their television screens or computers. Regrettably, many children today are starved of real-time friends and face-to-face interaction. Every minute their attention is absorbed in front of a screen is a minute they are not moving and playing.

It would not surprise me if some of today's children were to dial 911 if there was an emergency or spell colour without a "u", due to many American television shows permeating the airwaves at present.

It should be noted that our pocket money was quite limited. We could therefore not afford to stuff ourselves with sweets and crisps. Consequently, as we were much more physically active back then, there were not so many overweight children about.

I sometimes wonder if it is just a coincidence that current (2015, at the time of writing this paragraph) Scottish football and rugby teams are not producing nearly as many top players as they once did. Could it be that one of the major causes of this sad decline in playing standards is that children are deserting outside activities in record numbers for the comfort of indoor pursuits, and have much easier access to junk food?

4. Tenement life

For the first seven years of my life (1943-1950), I lived in a tenement flat at 92 Roxburgh Street, Greenock. These buildings were soot-encrusted tenements which were built in the 1920s and 1930s. They were finally demolished between the late 1950s and early 1960s, in order that more modern houses could take their place.

Figure 9 Bed-recess

The first-floor flat we lived in consisted of one bedroom, an outside toilet, and a large kitchen-cum-living room with a bed-recess. This type of bed, in which my young brother

Figure 10 Roxburgh Street

Martin and I slept in, was just a glorified large cupboard containing a double bed, with curtains on the outside.

The kitchen was a multi-function room where most of the daily activity took place. This was where you cooked, ate your meals, sat and listened to the radio, read the daily papers or books and, for many, slept. The coal fire was used for heating the room and in many cases cooked meals, boiled kettles and toasted bread. Most homes had little decoration. Utility furniture was the order of the day, plain, dark and uncomfortable. Very few homes had the luxury of a bathroom. For many, therefore, bath time was a large tin bath set up in the middle of the kitchen in front of a roaring fire (in winter). The area around the bath was surrounded with old newspapers scattered around the floor to catch escaping splashes of water.

**Figure 11 Weekly wash
in the   sink**

Alternatively, if you were small enough, you could be unceremoniously dumped in the kitchen sink and scrubbed into a state of scarlet cleanliness. Of course, every possible excuse was made to evade this, to us, appalling routine. After all, how could we possibly get dirty in just a week by playing outside in the streets and back greens? One of my friends recently told me that he complained bitterly to his mother that she had to stop washing him this way. When I asked him why he was so upset about it, he said it was because he was eighteen at the time. Mmmmm!

Although our tenement flat had electricity, the main room was lit by two gas mantles on either side of the fireplace wall. Great care had to be taken when inserting them into their holders as the mantles were extremely fragile due to the honeycombed silk material they were made from. If you so much as touched them with your lighted match they would disintegrate into dust. However, on the positive side, this material protected the gas jets

Figure 12
Gas Mantle

from crumbling and also helped to spread their light over a large area.

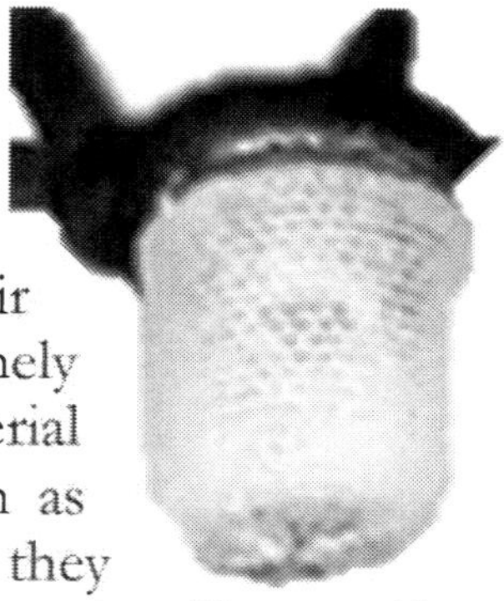

For decorative purposes, there was normally a glass cover screwed around them. The gas jets were lit with a match through a hole in the bottom of the glass globe, making sure that great care was taken not to touch the fragile mantle. When they were lit, a popping sound emanated from them. I am sure Health and Safety Regulations would severely restrict their use in modern houses today.

Our toilet was outside in the stairwell and was shared with another family who lived on the same first-floor level as us. In those days, there was none of your super-soft toilet paper for us. No, we used old newspapers torn into squares and nailed onto the wall beside the toilet door. Looking at it from a positive point of view, it meant that there was always something to read when waiting for nature to take its course. Some lucky or unlucky people, depending on your point of view, used Izal Germicide shiny toilet paper. However, as this was as useful as slippery tracing paper, it was of little help for the purpose it was designed for.

At least our family had a toilet on the stairwell, as many others were less lucky as their toilet facilities were outside, "doon the Dunny", beside the cellars.

As there was no heating, it would have tested the resolve of Scott of the Antarctic. Imagine, in the bleak winter months, having to put on a heavy hat, coat, boots, and if raining, carry an old umbrella before venturing out for a call of nature.

I've been reliably informed that early morning was the worst time of the day, as it

Figure 13 .
Outside Toilet

was not unusual for tenants to queue up to use this facility while they waited for their neighbour to finish their ablutions. Imagine the panic when you got to the door desperately needing some toilet relief, only to find an old lady or gentleman from the top flat had beaten you to it. It does not bear thinking about.

Italian poet Dante Alighieri once wrote, "All hope abandon, ye who enter here".in which he tells of his journey through Hell. This could well describe entering many of these outside toilets, as a gas mask and a strong constitution accurately describe what was needed before crossing the threshold of the outside toilet facilities many had to endure.

I recently read that the average man spends 394 days in the toilet throughout his life. If they had done this survey back in the days of outside toilets, I think 39.4 days would have been nearer the mark. Another report states that today 80 per cent of Scots like to read in the loo. If this analysis had been done back in those bygone days, I am sure you could have moved the decimal point two places to read 0.8 per cent instead. Especially as many of these out-houses had little or no light to illuminate the internal surroundings.

Therefore, a bizarre plus side was, as these amenities did not have electricity and were cold, gloomy places that often attracted small furry rodents and countless spiders etc., constipation very rarely reared its ugly head.

To save tenants from getting up in the middle of the night or first thing on a cold wet morning to pay a visit to the outside toilet, the trusty "chanty", or to give it its correct title, "chamber pot", was called into action. Although this was a very convenient way of relieving the burden within, there were not many volunteers forthcoming when an overflowing "chanty" needed to be carried out and then emptied down the nearest toilet.

I well remember being told the story of the poor housewife who tripped over a rug when carrying a full chamber pot. It was said that the screams of terror of her offspring could be heard for miles around as they shot out of the door before the contents even hit the floor.

*"When you get up in the morning, dinna blush with shame,
Remember your mother before you, did the very same."*

The most popular play areas for us kids then were the back greens of the tenement blocks. Looking back, I wonder why it was called a "green", as it was only a piece of barren brown dusty wasteland that never seemed to be cleaned up. However, this suited both parents and children, as we had plenty of independence which enabled us to run about and they had more peace and quiet indoors. In addition, it meant that parents could keep an eye on what their offspring were getting up to. Paradoxically, we certainly loved the freedom from parental guidance this freedom gave us.

This, of course, meant that the tenement window was a great communication portal between parents and children. An example of this technological innovation was when a mother wanted some items from the local corner shop. She would lean out of the window and throw down the money to her offspring, wrapped up in a note detailing what she required.

Windows were also our equivalent of a feeding tube. This came into operation when we were hungry and did not want to climb up flights of stairs just for something to eat. We would shout up to our mothers to "throw us doon a piece, please". That was the easy part, the hard part was trying to catch our piece of bread with butter and sugar splattered all over it, or a sickly sweet condensed milk sandwich, wrapped up in paper, as it plummeted down at a fair rate of knots. This was good practice for all the would-be goalkeepers, but a nightmare for today's dieticians.

One of the most important uses for tenement windows, in addition to their main function of trying to keep the elements at bay and letting light in, was using it as the equivalent of today's social media programmes. This entailed many women leaning out of their windows to relay the latest wedding or funeral gossip, or Mrs So-and So's operation, or the latest baby to enter the tenement world.

Please note that I'm not being sexist here, but I can't ever remember seeing any men passing the time of day using their open window to chatter away to their neighbours.

The tenement flats were so close to one another that it would have been a miracle if there had not been any clashes of personalities or misunderstandings that could last for weeks until a common bond of suffering or hardship brought the rival factions together again. Most of the men-folk didn't get involved with the feuds and went on nodding to each other when they met outside as though nothing untoward was happening.

This communal method of communication worked well when it was time for children's lunch or evening meal. To ensure they would be at the table when their meal was ready, mothers would shout out of the window, informing

Figure 14 Rag'n' Bone Man

them that their meal was sitting on the table. If the children were outwith earshot, other children who were within range would relay the message around the area until they were located and dispatched home. Yes, the tenement back green jungle drums were comparable to today's text messaging when it came to summoning children for their meals.

The tenements also attracted itinerant traders, who would come around touting their wares on a regular basis. As the buildings were clustered close together, they could entice a large number of people to buy their (sometimes dubious) merchandise without having to travel very far.

When I was a very young boy, my favourite trader was the Rag'n'bone man" who collected unwanted household items and sold them on to various merchants in order to make a small profit. Traditionally this was a task performed on foot, pushing a handcart. However, some of the more affluent rag'n'bone men used a pony and cart to collect unwanted goods.

Their modus operandi was to give a small toy or a few sweets to us kids in exchange for items our parents were throwing out. Woollen clothes were often top of their list, as they were the easiest to recycle. We did not care about whether this was an early Green recycling policy or not, as all we wanted were some old rags to exchange for sweets.

It was amazing how some mothers could produce old clothes whenever the Ragman appeared. In many ways, this was because she couldn't let her neighbours think her family was so

54

poor they couldn't even give her kids some rags for a few sweeties.

One of the most labour-intensive household chores for the tenement wife was the weekly washing, drying and ironing process. This was a period when tenement flats did not have running hot water, washing machines or tumble dryers, and there were few rubber gloves available to protect the skin from abrasive washing powder. Instead,

Figure 15 Communal Wash-house

many flats had a basement wash house where each household took turns at doing their weekly wash. Can you imagine what women's hands must have been like with all this manual washing? It was hard physical drudgery and, depending on the size of the family, could take all day to finish.

When each families' turn for the wash house key came around, they would start the process by lighting the boiler to heat the water.

The clothes were first scrubbed by hand, then fed through a hand-operated wringer which squeezed a large quantity of water out of articles such as towels, blankets, sheets and the family's clothes. Once this process was finished, the clean washing was hung out to dry on the communal outside drying green area. This was also done on a rota system, in order for all the tenants in the building to take advantage of the drying facilities.

Everyone, of course, hoped that when it was their turn for the weekly wash, the weather would be favourable so that their nice clean wash could be dried outside in the fresh air. Unfortunately, as the age of the tumble dryer was still in the distant future, it meant that when the weather was inclement, women

Figure 16 Drying Pulley

would have to hang their wet items inside the house on a pulley that consisted of a set of wooden hanging rails hoisted up to the ceiling by way of ropes, and well out of the way of children.

Housewives in tenements which didn't have wash-houses often took advantage of the purpose-built public ones which were available, and where they could take their weekly laundry too. When all the sinks were in use, it was said to look like the witches' scene in Macbeth, with the women in their headscarves and aprons, drenched in sweat, standing next to a cauldron of boiling water, which sat on a waist-high brick support encasing a roaring fire to keep the water boiling hot. All that was missing was their song

"Double, double toil and trouble;
Fire burn and cauldron bubble."

Some of these sinks were so large that it was jokingly said that small children would be able to dive into the water doing a double somersault in the pike position without reaching the bottom of the sink.

No wonder so many women aged well before their time, as they had very little respite from the constant physical exertion week after week, year after year. However, there were a multitude of books on sale (see an example in the picture opposite) explaining how to make their lives so much easier, as many of the books and articles advised women to leave their jobs and stay at home, as the accepted philosophy was that a woman's job was to bear and raise children

Figure 17 Home making book

I am sure many of the books would be considered quite misogynistic if their equivalent went on sale today. Indeed, there would no doubt be a social media petition raised, demanding that the authors of the said books be hung, drawn and quartered without mercy.

It is quite thought-provoking to note that in my lifetime we have come from the aforementioned drudgery for women, into the current washing and drying machine marvels that it is taken for granted today. Now, if only there had been a similar leap forward for mankind with the ironing.

It should be noted that housekeeping and raising a family were considered primarily female roles during the 1940s and '50s and indeed for countless generations prior to this period too. Men were thought of as the "breadwinners", and rarely helped with the household chores. This, of course, has now changed, mainly because a large percentage of women now also hold down full-time jobs. Back in my youth, many women were, before anything else, home-makers. From morning to evening, seven days a week, they burned off their calories labouring to feed and dress us kids and to keep us clean, safe and warm.

Almost every house was heated by coal which was delivered by lorry, and in some instances by horse and cart, with the coalmen shouting loud enough to awaken the dead "Yeeee-how" which we correctly

Figure 18 The Coalman

translated as "coal". The other combustible material that helped to keep the fires burning was Briquettes. These consisted of a compressed block of coal dust or combustible biomass material such as charcoal, sawdust, wood chips, peat, or paper used for fuel and kindling to start a fire. These were also shouted out by the coalman in their own inimitable manner. When I was very young, I would get quite excited when I heard their plaintive cry because I thought it was "old biscuits!" that they were shouting.

A pair of sturdy shoulders and strong legs (and a will to live, I think) were prerequisites for the men who carried the coal up to the top floor tenement flats.

It was no surprise that, when all the fires in the district were belching out smoke and fumes, almost everyone around joined in with a mass coughing and wheezing Olympics. However, I still have fond memories of sitting beside a roaring coal fire on a cold winter's night and using a long fork to toast our bread.

A dreadful consequence of all the burning coal fires was smog (an amalgam of the words "smoke" and "fog" used to refer to smoky fog). This pollution greatly reduced visibility and impaired respiratory function. Smog was prevalent in towns and

Figure 19 Real coal fire

cities until the introduction of the Clean Air Act of 1956, which introduced a number of measures to reduce air pollution, especially by introducing "smoke control areas" in some towns and cities in which only smokeless fuels could be burned.

To appreciate how hard work it was for the lady of the house, imagine it is 6.30 a.m. on a freezing cold winter morning and the single-glazed windows of your non-centrally-heated house are coated in ice, inside and outside. While we were still safely tucked up in our beds, many women would be down on their hands and knees cleaning out the now cold previous day's ashes from the living room fireplace, taking care not to cause a dust cloud that would obliterate vision down to about 3 feet. Once the dust had settled the fire was lit in order that at least one room would be nice and warm for their families when they got out of bed. After this was done, they would have to carry the ashes from the previous evening fire down to the backcourt "midden bins" so they would not be accidentally knocked over in the living room.

The ceremony for lighting the fire was another protracted procedure. Firstly, tightly screwed-up old newspapers were set on the bottom grill, then some sticks were laid crisscrossed on top of the newspapers. Next came the lumps of coal, which were strategically

Figure 20 Getting the fire started

positioned on top of the paper/firelighters. as it often needed some help to get it going.

This was when a trusty light metal cover, with a tactically placed handle (often made surreptitiously in the local shipyards and engine works), would be held over the fireplace opening to increase the draught under the fire. This was usually very effective, and you could then hear the fire roaring away behind the cover although, surprisingly enough, when the metal sheet was taken away, the fire seemed quite tame.

Families who did not have a metal cover would hold a sheet of old newspaper over the front of the fire in order to get a similar effect. It should be appreciated that this was a much more hazardous method because, as the draught increased, the newspaper could be sucked out of your hand and into the fire before shooting up the "lum", and, with a bit of luck, be vaporised before it shot out of the top of the chimney.

Unfortunately, many a chimney fire was caused by using this technique. However, one of the plus aspects of these particular fireplaces was that they were multi-purpose units, which often included a built-in oven(s) and hotplate (see the picture opposite).

Figure 21 Vintage fireplace with ovens

While the fire was being lit in the kitchen-cum-living room on a bitterly cold winter morning, I would poke my nose out from under the bedclothes and exhale a fine mist into the bitterly cold room air, which had often fallen to Siberian winter levels overnight. I would then look over at the window and admire the ice patterns that had formed on them. Next, I would kick the once lovely and hot, but now extremely cold, hot-water bottle quickly out of the bottom of the bed. Before the temperature rose to just above zero centigrade, a rolled-up tea towel was laid on the windowsills to soak up the water that dripped down the windowpanes as the room slowly thawed out.

The dread of putting my toes out onto the cold linoleum covered floor of the bedroom was overpowering. Therefore, the first thought that usually came into my head was how to persuade my mother that I had contracted a severe bout of the Black Death or some other dreadful disease during the night and would need to stay off school that day in order to recover.

Needless to say, this pitifully inadequate excuse fell on deaf ears. The blankets were deftly pulled from my foetal positioned little body as I was brusquely told, with the war cry heard to this very day, "I'll not tell you again, hurry up and get ready for school!" Yes, some things never change.

The aforementioned was the start of the average winter's day for many school children and housewives, as this was before the advent of central heating or electric/gas fires that can be turned on at the flick of a switch.

Many other household chores took up a lot of the woman of the houses time, because what was then considered "luxury" items, such as vacuum cleaners, washing machines, tumble dryers, electric irons, refrigerators and freezers, were way beyond the financial reach of the average family's budget. This, of course, meant that chores that are regarded today as inconsequential and a time-consuming nuisance were, in reality, a weekly, and in many cases a daily, arduous necessity.

5. A new era

After working for the Glebe Sugar Refinery, which is the free-standing, 1840 built, 5 storey red brick building situated at Ker Street, in 1951, my father was appointed to the position of senior maintenance engineer at the Rankin Memorial Maternity Hospital, which was originally opened on 17 August 1938, and closed and demolished in 1994. This was also the hospital I had been born in seven years before our move. The hospital was

Figure 22 The Rankin Hospital. Home from 1950 to 1960.

situated where the Rankin Rise housing scheme is now

Our new home was set in the hospital grounds and was situated in a semi-countryside area. It is worth noting that at this period in time, the Pennyfern, Branchton, Fancy Farm, Larkfield and Braeside housing schemes had not even been built. And the area they now occupy was just green fields and farmland.

This obviously meant a change from our old tenement flat to a nice little "tied cottage" in the grounds of the hospital, and was called "The Lodge". Although I was excited about our move to the Rankin Hospital, I was sorry to be leaving my many friends behind in the Roxburgh Street area.

I was seven years old at this time and had hardly ever seen green fields displaying various types of vegetation before. Indeed, the only cows and sheep I had seen previously were when they were being shepherded to the King Street abattoir, so the move was of epic proportions to me. You can imagine the culture shock it was for me as a young boy, moving from an old pre-WWII tenement flat situated in the middle of the town, which had an outside toilet and a set-in bed in the wall, to a cottage which, in those days, was more or less in the countryside.

The best thing about our new house was that my young brother Martin and I had our own bedroom to share. Our new home also had a bathroom/toilet. This was the very first time I had ever seen a room with a fitted bath, as previously we had to use a tin bath set up in our living room floor. It also had its own lovely garden, which was maintained by the Hospital's gardeners, and wonder of wonders, a private telephone. This last item was one of the most amazing objects I had ever seen close up, as the only other time I had ever seen one before was in the movies at our local cinemas or in a street Telephone Box.

I well remember the first time the telephone rang because I leapt over the back of the sofa and shot into the hall, where the telephone was situated, as fast as my little legs would take me to answer the phone. As can be appreciated, telecommunications have lost all their magic for me since that day way back in 1950 when I first clapped eyes on this large black Bakelite phone sitting on our new hall table. Young people today take for granted the immediate communication they have available to them. They can get in touch with their friends and family via computer, mobile phone or tablet almost instantly. Yes, sometimes the easiest way to communicate with your offspring in today's gadget world is by text, even if they are in the same room as you.

In addition, if the Internet goes down it is a young person's Code Red disaster. Indeed, you could find yourself being immediately reported to the Social Services for child neglect if you do not make a supreme effort get it up and running as quick as possible.

My childhood spent in "The Lodge", Rankin Hospital, from the early until the late 1950s, was one of the happiest periods of my life. We had large grass areas to play in, without the worry of heavy traffic thundering along the roads, or unsavoury characters wandering about the streets. I even managed to make some extra pocket-money from time to time by running errands for the ladies who were confined to the hospital.

As can be seen from the Visitor's Admission Card, visiting was restricted to the times detailed. Therefore, if any of the expectant mothers ran out of little tit-bits like biscuits, chocolate etc. they would shout out of the

RANKIN MEMORIAL HOSPITALS
MATERNITY WARDS.
Visitor's Admission Card.
Visiting Hour — 2.45 to 3.45pm
ON
SUNDAY, WEDNESDAY and SATURDAY
ADMISSION BY CARD ONLY

Only one visitor admitted at one time, and more than two during the hour.
No person under 16 allowed.

Telephone Enquiries: 9.00 — 10.00am and 6.00 — 7.00pm.

windows anytime I was passing, asking me if I would run a little shopping errand for them. Of course, if I was available I would jump on my bike and dash down to Johnnie Bruce's sweet-shop–cum-newsagents in the lane at Old Inverkip Road near the bottom of Grieve Road. These little errands often earned me about thruppence (1 ¼ pence in decimal money) for each trip.

As stated earlier, the drug culture in young people was practically unheard of. Instead, we loved to play outdoors on our bikes, or climb up the hills to The Cut to catch minnows and sticklebacks in jam jars. Not to mention playing football/cricket/rugby on every bit of spare ground we could find (anything to get us out of the house, I think). This is perhaps the major difference between my childhood and that of today's children because we were allowed out by ourselves. In fact, we seemed to be left to our own devices a lot of the time.

Although, as stated earlier, I missed my Roxburgh Street pals, I soon made new ones, as fortunately one of my old friend's, Iain Freer, had earlier moved to a "prefab" in Neil Street, which was very near to our new home. Iain soon introduced me to the boys and girls who lived in the area, so I blended into the local kids' scene quite quickly.

Iain's "prefab" home, as they were universally called, or to give them their proper name "Prefabricated Houses", were in abundance then, and were a vital answer to the housing shortage at the end of the Second World War. This was when a new, quick solution to the housing problem was needed, and needed urgently. Prefabs were overwhelmingly the preferred option to meet the housing shortage. And Greenock, like many other towns, had prefabricated homes which were manufactured off-site in advance, usually in standard sections that were easily shipped and quickly assembled. All approved prefab units had to have a minimum floor space size of 635 square feet (59.0 m2), and be a maximum of 7.5 feet (2.3 m) wide to allow for transportation by road

Furthermore, although the prefabs were just meant as transient housing, the facilities were far better than most of the tenement flats the occupiers had left. Almost all had a small garden, a separate bathroom and toilet (that is very rare, even today) and best of all for the children of the household – a refrigerator with a small freezer compartment. Ideal for making ice lollies.

Despite the original intention that these dwellings should be a strictly temporary measure, many of them remained inhabited for a

considerable period after the end of the War. My understanding is that there were still prefabs in use locally up to and including the 1960s.

Coincidentally, the prefab in the picture on the previou page was situated at the corner of Old Inverkip Road and Thom Street, and was on the opposite side of the street to my current home, where this particular paragraph was written.

Shopping was mainly the task of women and was a chore that had to be done almost every day, as freezers and refrigerators were still extremely rare, and the first microwave oven was not introduced until 1964/1966 by the Sharp Corporation of Japan. This meant that most women were slaves to the kitchen. Almost every meal had to be cooked from scratch, as there were no ready meals or fast food outlets back then.

To obtain the various food requirements it was normal practice to visit separate shops to buy bread (baker's), meat (butcher's), vegetables (greengrocer's) and fish (fishmonger's). The arrival of supermarkets, with all these items under one roof, was still a long way into the future. However, it should be noted that, on the plus side, shopping was a great social networking opportunity long before Facebook and Twitter came into existence, as all the latest local news (an obvious euphemism for gossip) was speedily passed around on a regular basis.

A popular shop that always seemed to be located near where a high density of people lived was the local Cooperative (Co-op) shop. It was unique in many ways as it allowed many ordinary people to shop on credit terms. And it gave back a small percentage of the price of the goods purchased in the form of a "dividend". Customers were "members" of the Co-op, each with their own exclusive "share" number (which many people could still remember decades after the dividend system ceased to exist).

After the purchase, this unique number was given to the shopkeeper, who would note it down and give a carbon copy slip back to the customer as proof of purchase. Members could choose when the dividend payday was. A period in time was usually selected when the extra money would be very useful, such as the start of the school year when children's new uniforms would be required, or at Christmas/New Year time.

Amongst the "gadgets" that used to fascinate me in the Co-op, and many larger shops. was the Cash Carrier, as they were used in shops and department stores to carry customers' payments from the sales assistant to the cashier's office, and then carry any change and receipt back again. The payment was carried in a small tube along a suspended ceiling-located carriage

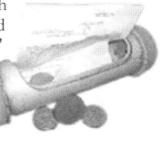

Figure 24 Cash Carrier

system which ran down a wire at a considerable rate of knots from the Sales Assistant's desk to the Cashier's secured office. The obvious advantage was that there was no need to keep cash in shop floor cash registers. This also prevented any light-fingered thieves from plying their unsavoury trade.

A similar method of transferring cash to the Accounts Department was by pneumatic tube. With a sudden whoosh, this device sent the sales slip and money in a vacuum tube through the extended cylinder to the Cashier's office. The change came back by the same method. Some shops and supermarkets still use an updated version of this method of collecting cash deposits.

It should be noted that payment for goods was normally made by cash or cheque. Hire purchase was sometimes available if the total price of the goods was outwith the buyer's immediate budget, as Credit and Debit Cards had not yet been introduced by the banks at this time (see the next chapter for further details).

7. Banks

It should be noted that, back in the 1950s, Britain was largely a cash-driven society, as almost every transaction was made with ready money, in full, or else on "the never-never" in weekly or monthly instalments. As stated in the previous chapter, Credit Cards did not exist in the 1950s. (The Barclaycard was the first credit card introduced in the UK, coming into use in 1966, and it enjoyed a monopoly until the introduction of the Access card in 1972.)

It should be appreciated that the working culture was not really geared up to paying wages into a bank account, as many people didn't have one back in those days. Most people were therefore paid in cash on a Friday, usually in a little brown envelope with holes punched in the side which enabled you to check the number of notes before you opened the wage packet. The idea behind this procedure was to ensure that if the payee claimed he or she had not been paid the correct amount, they could show that the pay envelope was still unopen. If the pay packet had been opened, there was no way of proving that they had not taken out some money before complaining of being short paid.

Unfortunately, it was not unknown for a percentage of this cash to have been deposited with the local bookmaker and public house landlords long before some men had returned home, sometimes a little the worse for wear. Because of this, some housewives waited at the factory gates to relieve their husbands of their wages before they had the chance to spend them in their favourite watering hole. As a matter of interest, it should be noted that the standard rate of income tax was an eye-watering nine shillings (45 per cent) in the pound – more than twice the rate today (2018).

In today's modern world, some people consider banks to be the spawn of Satan following the financial crisis of 2007/2008 and the challenging fiscal legacy that it left many people with. However, when I was young, banks were quite austere places for the general public to visit. Long queues were not uncommon, and the privilege of withdrawing your hard-earned cash was often restricted to the branch of the bank that the money had been deposited in. Even trying to make a withdrawal from another branch of the same bank in the same town could be a problem. Worse still, almost every other bank in the civilised world was off-limits to you, except for the one that you had deposited your cash into.

Indeed, a Court Order was almost required when we had the temerity, nay, the effrontery, to try and withdraw our money from our own bank, but in a different town or city. Obviously, I am exaggerating a bit here, but you should get my gist.

An example of this could be if we happened to run short of cash in some far-flung exotic holiday resort such as Largs, Millport or Rothesay. Sometimes the normal riposte from the cashier was, "Do you have an arrangement with this bank, Sir/Madam?" While we were often tempted to say "No, but I'm Al Capone, so stick 'em up, sucker!". Instead, we would have to bite our tongue and think better of it, as sarcasm would not be appreciated while we pleaded for our own money to stave off starvation.

If we were fortunate enough to pass the interminable set of questions we were given, our own money was then released into our custody. Once, when leaving the bank, a friend, who had been waiting for me outside for quite a while said "Where have you been? Christmas wasn't the same without you. Your grandchildren missed you as well". "Grandchildren? What grandchildren? I didn't have any when I went into the bank" Obviously, again I have just made this up, but it is a metaphor for what seemed like a lifetime it took to withdraw our own hard-earned money.

Maybe I am being a little harsh with the previous comments because, in those days, banks meant reliability. Their traditional fixtures and fittings were as reassuringly strong as the handshake of a favourite friend or relative wishing you a happy birthday. Whereas today the financial scandals that followed the effects of the crash of 2007/2008 have destroyed the solid image the banks once had when the "movers and shakers" of investment banking shifted their priorities from serving customers to pleasing shareholders and their determination to rise to global prominence.

Concerning this irritation, we should all thank a Scottish inventor named John Shepherd-Barron who led the team that installed the first cash machines, sometimes referred to as the automated teller machine or ATM. The first one was used on June 27, 1967. Incidentally, this was 50 years to the day since I wrote this particular paragraph.

I note that today (2018) many banks are now phasing out their least used ATM's and High Street branches because so many people are now using internet banking and are therefore slowly turning us into a cashless society.

8. Street lights

The street lights and stairwells back in the 1940/'50s around the Roxburgh Street area where I grew up in were powered by gas and were lit every night at twilight by a "leerie". Leeries were lamplighters whose job was to ensure the streets were illuminated at night.

Out in all kinds of weather, they used a long pole which had a naked flame at the tip that would light each mantle. A blue spluttering flame would burst into life, followed by a brilliant white, spreading arc of welcoming light. This was often the signal for us kids that it was time for our recreation period to cease for the evening, and that we should return home – very reluctantly, I might add. As dawn broke, the leeries had to trudge back to all the lights they had switched on in order to switch them back off again. The last gas stairwell and street lights were dismantled in 1961.

My tea is nearly ready and the sun has left the sky;
It's time to take the window to see the Leerie going by;
For every night at teatime and before you take your seat
With lantern and with ladder he comes posting up the street.

Now Tom would be a driver and Maria go to sea,
And my papa's a banker and as rich as he can be;
But I, when I am stronger and can choose what I'm to do,
O Leerie, I'll go round at night and light the lamps with you!

For we are very lucky, with a lamp before the door,
And Leerie stops to light it as he lights so many more;
And oh! before you hurry by with ladder and with light;
O Leerie, see a little child and nod to him tonight!

Robert Louis Stevenson

Figure 25 The Leerie

9. Personal transport

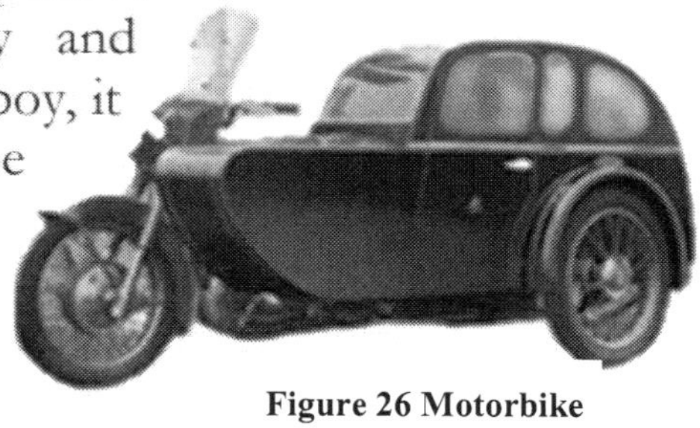

As cars were a very expensive mode of transport to buy and maintain when I was a young boy, it meant that if a mechanical type of transportation was required, then a motorbike was a much more economical and reliable method of transport that would fit the bill.

Figure 26 Motorbike and Sidecar

My grandfather, father and two maternal uncles were great enthusiasts of this method of transport in their formative years. Indeed, they used to repair and build them in their spare time. In addition to this, my grandfather, Joseph Bolton, was also a great supporter of the yearly Isle of Man TT Motorcycle Races and went to see them race on numerous occasions. An early "Hell's Angel" methinks my old Granddad was.

My initial recollections (circa 1950) of this manner of transport were of a motorcycle and sidecar my Dad and Mum had, which was very similar to the one in the picture above. For those readers who have never seen a sidecar, it is a one-wheeled device attached to the side of a motorcycle Up until the 1950s sidecars were a quite popular and cheap alternative to motor cars. I recently read that when driving one of these motorcycles the laws of physics went flying out of the window. Nevertheless, my four-year-old young brother Martin and I used to squeeze into the sidecar and off our family would go to exotic faraway destinations like Lunderston Bay and Largs. Happy days.

10. Outside recreation

One of our favourite play areas was the Well Park in Regent Street. The Well (see picture below), which gave the park its name and is still standing, was erected by the then local laird John Shaw in 1629.

When I look back to these sublimely happy and peaceful days, the sun always seemed to shine when we were there. Soaring high on the swings and swirling around on the roundabouts. Not forgetting watching the old worthies playing draughts on the large board marked out on the ground. Ah!

Figure 28 Well Park - circa 1955

Figure 27 Well Park - 2014

happy days again.

It should be noted that we were only about five or six years old at the time, and we were allowed, and indeed encouraged, to go and play in the park on our own or with friends while our parents were at work or at home catching up with the housework This certainly wouldn't be contemplated today. Young children of that age playing in a park without supervision a half mile from their home? I don't think so.

One of the downsides to these halcyon days was that I seemed to be injury-prone, because in addition to the usual cuts and bruises we kids got playing cowboys and Indians etc., I broke my right arm in 1947

Figure 29 The "Well"

when I tripped over a fence-post (detailed earlier), then in 1949 I broke my left arm when I fell down a flight of stairs. Tests were taken to see if I had some form of brittle bone syndrome. Thankfully it turned out this was not the case, as it appears I was just careless and a little bit unlucky when out playing.

Being young children during this period, we did not appreciate that there could be a better way of life. We also did not realise some houses had gardens and inside toilets. Parents couldn't reach us (no mobile phones in those days) unless we were within shouting distance playing in the back greens of the tenements. However, they knew we would be safe since there were very few undesirable individuals ("numpties", in the Scottish vernacular) wandering the streets in daylight under the influence of banned substances or alcohol.

We also played on the paved side streets, as there was very little motor traffic about, although some horse-drawn carts still pounded along the cobbled roads.

To keep us amused we even collected car registration numbers (Greenock's started with the letters "VS" until 1974). then we wrote them down in our little notebooks as they drove past us in Roxburgh Street and compared them later with our pals. In those bygone days, we would be lucky to collect a couple of dozen in an hour. Today, we would miss that many while we were writing the number plates down in our little notebooks. We would also have the local Special Branch no doubt asking what we were up to, into the bargain!

A scramble (or scrammy) wedding in the street was a magnet for all the kids in the surrounding area. It was a tradition that the people in the bridal car (usually the father of the bride), would toss a shower of small denomination coins out of the car window for good luck, as they left for the wedding ceremony. This caused an almighty scramble which left many children with skinned knees and sore knuckles, as it was a potential monetary bonanza for us kids that would make us rich, for that day at least.

74

To understand the excitement this caused, you have to picture a Scotland *v.* England rugby scrum free-for-all to appreciate the mayhem that was caused in the mad dash to collect as many halfpennies, pennies and maybe even thrup-penny bits from the roadside as we could get. Trying to fend off the other kids by fair means or foul was an art form in itself. All

Figure 30 Scrammy Wedding - circa 1950

the coins would be eagerly collected and taken to the shops for the "penny tray" of sweets, or maybe even the tuppenny or thruppenny tray if you had a really good scrammy.

Hallowe'en on 31st October was one of our favourite times of the year. This was when we would paint our faces and dress up in bizarre home-made outfits and go out in the evening to entertain any household that would let us over their threshold in order to perform our little jokes and poems. The most common costumes for boys were either a cowboy outfit we had received the previous Christmas, or alternatively dressing up as our Dad, complete with a flat-top bunnet and working jacket that was five sizes too big. Finally, a painted-on moustache and an old clay pipe made up our regalia for the evening's show. Today's children call this ritual by the Americanism "Trick or Treat", but to our generation in Greenock, it was always "going out in Galoshins".

It should be noted that today's children are usually driven to their prearranged appointments by their proud parents and wear expensive costumes which were hired or bought for the occasion. Not for us! The evening started when we would leave our homes at predetermined times and meet up with our itinerant friends, all ready for an evening of high expectation and hope that we would return later loaded down with a generous bag of treats. It should be noted here that adults were strictly taboo on our nomadic ramblings throughout our local area.

When our little group of troubadours were gathered together, off we would go to knock on the doors of neighbours we knew, hoping that they were not fed up with other Galoshins who had beaten us to their house. When we did manage to convince householders, it would be to their benefit to let us entertain them, our little concert party would perform their previously rehearsed acts, which were usually greeted with polite applause, whether we were good or bad. The rewards for our artistic endeavours were often some fruit, a little bag of nuts and a few coppers each that we immediately transferred into a small bag we carried which held all our goodies.

After we had trawled all the known houses, we would cast our nets wider to see if we could persuade some less familiar households that they should let the best little group of entertainers they would get that evening into their houses. Could you envisage that happening today? Young children knocking on strangers' doors asking to come in? I think not.

At the end of the evening, we would count how much money, sweets and fruit we had each accumulated for our few hours of theatre. A monetary value above two shillings (10p) was deemed to be the equivalent of winning today's National Lottery and would be the talk of the school the next day.

Yes, we had great times then, back in the days of innocence. However, I don't doubt that the children of today enjoy their yearly Hallowe'en or Trick or Treat performances just as much as we did.

Our next highlight came a few days after Hallowe'en when, on 5th November, we remembered Guy Fawkes and his cohorts unsuccessful attempt to blow up the Houses of Parliament in 1605, by celebrating Bonfire Night (see Chapter 21, "Secondary school education", for more information).

In the days leading up to the fifth, we often built an effigy of Mr Fawkes made from straw or rags and dressed it in old clothes that were no longer wanted. We then placed the dummy in a wheelbarrow or old pram and pushed it around the neighbourhood hoping to raise a few pennies that would go towards buying fireworks.

Figure 31 Box of Fireworks

Fireworks normally appeared in the shops a couple of weeks before 5th November. Selection boxes dominated our choice as they held various types of fireworks (the most popular brands were Standard Fireworks and Brock's Fireworks). Alternatively, single rockets and larger fireworks could be purchased separately. Catherine wheels and Roman candles were particularly popular, as were sparklers and bangers (or squibs, as we called them).

We would let off our little boxes of fireworks in the nearest piece of waste ground, then troop off to the closest bonfire to carry on with our celebrations. These bonfires would give today's Health and Safety officers apoplexy, as they were normally organised by the parents of children who lived in the area surrounding where the bonfire was built.

Figure 32 5th November Bonfire

Bonfire parties and get-togethers with the neighbours were very popular. As for health and safety: well, apart from an annual safety lecture on BBC television's "Blue Peter", good old common sense was the order of the day.

Apart from playing with our pals, entertainment was quite limited to reading and radio broadcasts from the BBC, a lot of which must honestly be said that young kids found quite boring. In the early '50s business magnets were always looking for new ways to entertain the masses. Occasionally, nomadic entertainers would appear at local halls, trying to brighten up the lives of the populace. These included strongman acts, when the audience was invited to surpass the star of the show by lifting weights and bending iron bars etc.

One event I well remember was sneaking into one of the many local social halls in Greenock to see a certain Syncopating Sandy. Sandy's claim to fame was that he travelled the length and breadth of the country playing the piano non-stop for over 100 hours, in his attempt to set a new world record. (Not that anyone really knew if there was such a thing. And did he set a new world record everywhere he went we wondered?) Can you imagine today paying out hard earned money to go and see a man or woman playing an instrument continuously for hour after hour? Yes, we were NOT spoiled by a proliferation of entertainment when I was a young boy.

Before the wireless came along, my parents listened to crystal sets (or cat's whisker receivers, as they were often called) that could only be listened to with headphones. These crystal radios were a very simple type of radio receiver and were made with a few inexpensive parts, such as a wire for an antenna, another coil of wire, a capacitor, a crystal detector, and earphones. Because of its limitations, this obviously meant that only one person at a time could listen to it. I remember my mother telling me that when she was a young girl (which would have been the late 1920s), a clever friend of her older brothers had built a crystal set himself. And as this was the only one in the surrounding district, she said he had a full house almost every night of the week, with people eager to hear a few minutes each of the BBC on his headphones.

So the crystal wireless, even with the above-mentioned power limitations, was still a great improvement on the crystal sets as it had, amongst other modifications, an inbuilt speaker that let all the family hear the programmes together.

Therefore, the "wireless" in those early days really was wire less. Why did most of us of a certain age call it a wireless? Well, the only power it had was a high-tension battery and an accumulator (an apparatus by means of which energy was stored

Figure 33
Accumulator

- pictured opposite). When the power ran out, it had to be taken to a radio retailers shop where they would put the depleted accumulator on an electric charge overnight. We would then collect it the next day, along with the usual verbal message "Remember, don't shake it about or you'll mix up your radio stations!" ringing in our ears. I'm sure some people actually believed that this was a fact.

This was leading-edge technology at its best, 1940s style. Imagine taking your iPad or smartphone to your local electrical retailer every time the battery needed to be charged.

Why was it not just plugged into a wall power socket you may ask? The reason for this dates back to the period before World War II when the coverage by the Central Electricity Grid, which was set up in 1935 and supplied Britain's homes, was a long way short of completing its task. Even by the third year of the war, as many as

one-third of Britain's homes were not connected to the grid. Therefore, to ensure a continuous signal, radios were not plugged into the mains but powered by accumulators/batteries.

In the mid-1940s, we eventually got a "wireless" which really had a wire that plugged into the wall instead of the infamous accumulator described earlier. The large tuning dial on the front of the wireless detailed all sorts of exotic faraway places. As the dial was turned, a lot of crackling and distorted sounds assailed your ears until the required station was located. There were no fancy push-button FM or DAB radio stations then.

To ensure that the householder was not listening for free, a licence fee of £1 a year had to be paid to the BBC before you could legally listen to the radio.

In the 1950s there were three main BBC radio stations broadcasting in Britain. The most widely listened to service was the "Light Programme", which brought us popular entertainment shows such as *Music While You Work* (1940-

Figure 34 Radio Licence

1967). Each half-hour show featured a different band playing a non-stop medley of popular middle-of-the-road tunes. A similar kind of show was *Workers' Playtime* (1941-1964). This was morale-boosting music, comedy and variety show which was broadcast live at weekday lunchtimes from factory canteens all over Britain, and ran for 23 years.

However, for younger teenage audiences, one of the most popular programmes was broadcasted on Saturday mornings, when Brian Matthew introduced *Saturday Club* (1958-1969). Brian chatted with guest artists in the studio and introduced their live performances, often before they had even established themselves as recording stars. Almost every pop star in Britain appeared on the programme, which was always broadcast live. There was also plenty of mainstream light entertainment in the form of variety shows, comedy and drama. For drama, it was Charles Chilton's *Journey into Space* with the intrepid space commander Jet Morgan and his motley crew. Listening recently to excerpts from this radio show, I soon realised that the story and sound effects were pretty tame compared to today's *Dr Who* epics, but back in the 1950s we were hiding behind the settee (even though it was on the radio) when Jet and his crew found themselves in mortal danger.

For younger listeners, there were the "Aunts" and "Uncles" of *Children's Hour*, which was broadcasted every day from 5 pm to 6 pm and was aimed at an audience aged from about 3 to 10 years.

Amongst the comedy shows we enjoyed listening to were *Ray's a Laugh, The Clitheroe Kid, Life with the Lyons* and, strangest of all, *Educating Archie* (which won the *Daily Mail's* National Radio Award three years running – 1951, 1952, 1953).

The radio show attracted up to 15 million listeners and had a children's fan club that at one time had 250,000 members. Why strange? Well, you see, Archie was a ventriloquist's dummy! On the wireless! What we wanted to know was whether Peter Brough, who was Archie's ventriloquist, was moving his lips when speaking Archie's lines? A bizarre episode in Archie's career happened in 1951 when he was kidnapped. Millions

Figure 35 Educating Archie- with Peter Brough

followed the story in the press as if he was a real child. Eventually, the person responsible for stealing Archie sent an anonymous note saying that Archie could be found at the Lost Property Office at London's King's Cross Station. The nation held its breath then rejoiced as Archie was reunited with Mr

Brough. You couldn't make up a story about an incident like that today, or could you?

After ten successful radio years, *Educating Archie* finally made the transition from the Light Programme to television in the 1950s, but it was a resounding flop, as Mr Brough didn't realise that ensuring your lips did not move was a prerequisite for a ventriloquist. Imagine our disappointment when we saw his lips moving in time with Archie's! Needless to say, Mr Brough's career soon went into immediate meltdown.

Radio quiz shows were few and far between back in the 1950s. However, one of the favourites was *Have a go* with Wilfred Pickles. It ran from 1946 right up to 1967. The weekly jackpot prize was an eye-watering thirty-four shillings (£1.85 in decimal money) with smaller prizes of 2/6d (12.5p) for runners-up. Yes, the BBC sure knew how to splash out the licence payer's money when I was a lad.

Next, there was the "Home Service", which also had its fair share of general entertainment programmes. However, this was the main channel for news, features and drama of a more demanding kind. It was also the station of regional programming.

Lastly came the "Third Programme" which was unashamedly highbrow in character, and was only broadcast in the evenings. Its output consisted of classical music concerts, recitals, and talks on matters scientific, philosophical and cultural, together with poetry readings and classic or experimental plays. Strangely enough, I can't remember anyone in our family tuning into this station. Its equivalent today is Radio 3, which many of its aficionados would listen to even if it was broadcasting the shipping forecast for Iceland.

The other radio station we regularly tuned in to was "Radio Luxembourg", which was the first commercial radio station we had ever heard and only broadcasted in the evening (whenever we could get a decent signal). Amongst the favourite programmes we boys listened to in rapturous silence were *Dan*

Dare: Pilot of the Future, and *Dick Barton – Special Agent*. After listening to these programmes in the evening, we could not wait to get to school the next morning to debate how Dan and Dick were going to deal with the dastardly deeds that had befallen them the previous evening.

This station was also our first introduction to almost non-stop pop music, as the BBC at this time concentrated in the main on middle-of-the-road, easy-listening ballad singers such as Frank Sinatra, Perry Como, Bing Crosby, Dean Martin, Peggy Lee, Rosemary Clooney etc., all crooning about finding and losing love. Whereas all we wanted to hear was rock 'n' roll heaven with stars like Elvis Presley, Buddy Holly and Little Richard. Yes, American rock'n'roll hit us like a thunderbolt. .Even now, when people of our mature generation are feeling frail and a little tired, it only takes the wailing saxophone introduction of Paul Anka's Diana to take us back to our school days again amongst our friends, and with all our loves and lives still ahead of us.

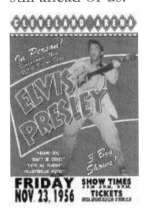  

In 1948 my education started at the Holmscroft School, which was located at the junction of Dempster Street and Ann Street. Its foundation stone had been laid in 1887 and the school was demolished in 1968. So it was already over 60 years old when I started my studies. We all have memories of our first day at school and the apprehension we

Figure 36 Classroom - circa 1950

felt as the big day finally arrived. This was the first time we were on our own, away from home in a regulated environment, as there were no state pre-schools or nurseries in the 1940s that prepared us for a formal education.

However, we soon got over the first pangs of separation, and school life soon fell into a predictable routine where new friendships were quickly made.

This was in the days when pupils sat two to a desk, which was bolted to the stepped floor – boys with boys, girls with girls. The desks, which had been in use for at least 60 years prior to my arrival, had a hole for an inkwell and a slot for a pencil. Under the surface of the sloping desk was a ledge for our personal gear, which was mainly our "play-piece". All the boys wore short trousers, which fell to just above our knees, and long grey woollen socks held up by elastic garters, which were expected to be pulled up to just below our bare knees, whether it was summer or winter.

Back in those innocent days, no self-respecting mother would send her children to school without their play-piece. This was usually a sandwich or a biscuit, which was eaten during the mid-morning break/playtime. And, oh my, it was a Code Red disaster if you forgot to take it with you when you left home, as it meant a rumbling stomach until lunchtime unless one of your pals relented to your constant pleading of "go on, gie's a bit of your piece, please".

There was also a free 1/3rd of a pint of milk scheme in force. Every morning we were all given a small bottle of milk from a wire crate to supplement our play-piece. The milk nearly always had about an inch of cream at the top and was slightly warm by the time we got it – ugghh! My understanding is that this scheme was discontinued in 1971 by Margaret Thatcher, the then Secretary of State for Education.

At lunchtime, I ran down Ann Street to my home in Roxburgh Street in about two minutes flat, had my midday meal, and then took about half an hour to reluctantly trudge back up the hill to school for the afternoon lessons (no parental school runs in those days).

Although I usually went home for lunch, I sometimes stayed for school dinners, which were of a rudimentary nature, simple and filling. The food was typical 1940s and 1950s fare: meat and two vegetables, or alternatively, macaroni cheese. After munching our way through our main course came a dessert such as rice pudding, semolina, tapioca or jam sponge and custard. A downside to school dinners then was that children were expected to clear their plates and were told off in no uncertain terms if they didn't.

I have very happy memories of the two-and-half years I spent at the Holmscroft School, and although school discipline was quite strict, we all benefited from it. We were very respectful to the teachers and were made to behave ourselves. "Don't fidget! Sit up straight! Fold your arms!" was a regular command from our teachers. However, this firm regime appeared to work, as it was very rare for anyone to step out of order. In view of this discipline, we all seemed to learn quite quickly. Fundamental knowledge of the three Rs – 'riting, 'rithmetic and reading – was soon drummed into us.

One of the first things that starting school taught me was that there were different religious beliefs in the country, as I could not understand why some of my good friends were not in the same class as me, even though we were all about the same age and lived on the same street.

At the end of my first day there, my parents told me the reason why some of my friends were not in my class at school that day was because they were of a Catholic religion, and I was a Protestant, therefore, we would need to attend different schools. This was a bit unsettling for all of us, but our friendships continued in spite of this segregation. It's quite sad that even now, over 70 years later, very little has changed regarding this situation

As stated earlier, it should be noted that there was no nursery provision for pre-school children. They, therefore, stayed at home with their mothers as it was quite rare for mothers to work and fathers to be domesticated until they were old enough to start school.

**Figure 38 Holmscroft School- Yours
truly 6th from the left in the middle row.**

As mentioned earlier, in 1951, my father was appointed to the position of senior maintenance engineer at the Rankin Memorial Maternity Hospital. This meant that I had to change school to one in a different catchment area. As we had moved house during the school term, I still had to attend the Holmscroft School in Ann Street until the first-holiday recess. This meant that I had to catch a scheduled bus each morning from the corner of Inverkip Road and Neil Street to the West Station and then walk the mile-and-a-half uphill to the Holmscroft School in Ann Street. This procedure was obviously reversed when it was time to make my own way home. This was quite an adventure for me, as I had only just turned eight years old at the time, and had to make this journey on my own because my mother had to stay at home to look after my four-year-old brother Martin. Can you imagine this happening today?

I noted that a recent survey by the Policy Studies Institute at Westminster University indicated that in 1971, 75 per cent of school children travelled to school alone (I'm sure that in the 1950s this percentage would have been much higher), whereas today this has dropped to 25 per cent. The survey argues "today's primary school children lead highly restrictive lives compared to kids 40 years ago". Unfortunately, this reflects badly on the society we now live in.

After the first holiday recess, I was eventually transferred to the Lady Alice School in Inverkip Road. I thoroughly enjoyed the next five years there, and it was where I made many new friends. This was also where I first met my future wife, Marion Nimmo. However, in those days' boys and girls normally kept to themselves and were segregated in class and in the playground. Girls in rows of desks at the left hand of the classroom. And boys at the right-hand side, so Marion and I rarely, if ever, acknowledged each other's existence back then.

Although the Lady Alice School was a much more modern school, being built in 1937, than the circa 1888 built Holmscroft School that I had just left, the desk arrangements, with the pupils sitting two to a desk and in rigid stepped lines – boys with boys, girls with girls – were just the same as the much older Holmscroft School.

The seating arrangements were also regulated by test marks. The brightest pupils were seated to the top left and the educationally challenged to the bottom right at their side of the class. Therefore, everyone knew who the cleverest was and who the unfortunate "dunderheids" were. I suppose one of the reasons for this system was to make the pupils who were lower down the pecking order aspire to improve their educational prowess. However, this is one system that is rightly consigned to the annals of history.

Another discriminatory policy was the school dinners mentioned earlier. Free school meals were available for children with families on low incomes. Whereas all other children paid a relatively small amount of money for their dinners. This, of course, meant that the class knew who could and could not afford to pay for their meal. Note that I use the word "dinners", as the expression "lunch" was rarely used in the UK back in the 1940s and 50s.

Although there was a considerable difference in the ages of the two schools, one thing they had in common was the teaching methods they used. During my period at school, Primary and Secondary, teachers didn't have the visual aids they have now, such as computers, iPads or instructional television programmes to explain the intricacies of reading, writing and arithmetic. No, they relied almost totally on the chalkboard and chalk, allied to their own strength of character, to get their message across.

Back in my school days, (1948 - 1958) if you were often off sick during term time it was possible that there would be a visit from the "School Board man", whose job was to ascertain whether you really were off sick or just malingering. This meant that if the child was not at home when he called to check on the absentee pupil, then the wrath of the School Board would descend from a great height upon parents if they did not have a legitimate excuse for the child being absent without permission.

Yes, truancy was severely frowned upon, and strictly dealt with. The aforementioned "School Board men" would prowl the parks and streets looking for "skidgers" (which was the colloquial name for pupils who had decided to take time off school for no particular reason). Punishment for both parent and child could be quite severe and, if the practice was habitual, children could be sent to a Borstal detention centre as a punishment

School holidays were greatly valued, as they still are now, especially the six-week summer ones. Other holidays were few and far between compared with today. In addition to the summer holidays, we had Easter, Christmas and New Year Holidays, but that was about it. None of the "special days", "mid-term days", "teacher training days" and "study days" that cause some working parents today to go into a panic trying to arrange for available family member or friends to look after their offspring until the holiday was over.

One of my biggest school regrets, while I attended the Lady Alice School, was not my educational progress, which was acceptable, but a sporting disaster

Figure 39 Murdieston Football Pitch

rivalling Scotland's 9-3 defeat by the "Auld Enemy" England in 1961.

It was when I was almost twelve years old, and in my last primary year at school. This was when I enjoyed my '15 minutes of fame, well a couple of minutes anyway' as I scored, with only a few minutes of the game to go, the only goal of the match for the school in the semi-final of the Greenock & District Schools' Cup. However, crushing disappointment followed when I broke my leg playing rugby a few days before the final (which the school went on to win without me, I might add). I've told this story to my nearest and dearest so many times that they scream and dive for cover behind the nearest obstacle they can find every time I start to mention it. So that's why I've deliberately attached a photograph of a re-enactment of the goal of the 20th Century, with my Granddaughter Rhianna Goodall hitting the ball so fast that it shot past my Grandson Justin Goodall and I before we could even move.

I have, of course, made light of the time I scored this goal, but I can still remember it as if it was yesterday with the raw passion it aroused, with all my school teammates diving on top of me, screaming "GOAL!"

Seriously, I think there is little difference between me scoring a goal that propelled a bunch of young schoolboys into a cup final for the first, and perhaps only time in their lives, and a professional footballer scoring the winner in a national cup final. Financially, of course, but emotionally and passionately, there is little difference at all.

In the 1955 Lady Alice group school picture of Primary 7, I am second from the left in the back row and Marion Nimmo, who I later married in 1964 and spent 40 very happy years with, is

Figure 40 Lady Alice School- 1954. 2nd from left, back row.

the fourth girl from the right in the second back row.

It's 1955 and I'm 12 years old. This was the period in school when we all sat our Scottish Qualifying Exam or "Qualy", as it was more commonly called. The results of your "Qualy" exam determined whether you were to progress to the Greenock High School (GHS) Senior Secondary School in Dunlop Street, with its emphasis on academic subjects such as Mathematics, History, Geography, English and languages, or go to the Mount Junior Secondary School for boys in Trafalgar Street or to the Finnart School in Newton Street (later to become the Ardgowan Primary School) for girls. Both of these schools concentrated on more artisan pursuits. in addition to the three Rs: of Reading, wRiting and aRithmetic.

As today, primary school teachers were charged with teaching us everything, from spelling and painting to world geography and mathematics. In addition to all this, they were like the Google of their time, trying to answer every question we threw at them. Moving on to secondary school teachers, they focused on individual subjects they were disciplined in.

Fortunately, I managed to pass my "Qualy" exam, more by good luck and guesswork than educational prowess and spent the next three years at the GHS (which was on the same site in Dunlop Street as Notré Dame High School is now).

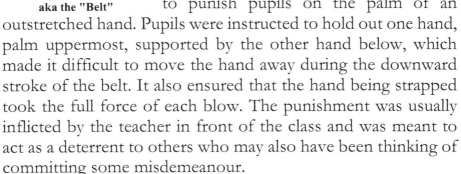

Whilst I thoroughly enjoyed my time at both the Holmscroft and Lady Alice primary schools, I admit that I just about tolerated my period at the Greenock High, as I couldn't help but feel my future life did not require my in-depth knowledge of Algebra, Latin Verbs, Shakespeare

Figure 41 The Greenock High School

quotations, and French literature etc.

It is worth noting that in the senior secondary schools the boys and girls were completely segregated during lessons and playtime.

In the years mentioned previously, corporal punishment for misdemeanours was still used, for both boys and girls, even in junior primary schools. In Scottish public (state) schools, the tawse, or "the belt" or "strap", as we called it, was used

Figure 42 The Tawse aka the "Belt"

to punish pupils on the palm of an outstretched hand. Pupils were instructed to hold out one hand, palm uppermost, supported by the other hand below, which made it difficult to move the hand away during the downward stroke of the belt. It also ensured that the hand being strapped took the full force of each blow. The punishment was usually inflicted by the teacher in front of the class and was meant to act as a deterrent to others who may also have been thinking of committing some misdemeanour.

My memories of a few of the teachers in both junior primary school and senior secondary school back in the 1940s and 50s aren't good. While there were many pleasant, well-respected teachers, there was a minority of austere, usually middle-class ladies and gentlemen, who ruled with a rod of iron, and who were no doubt brought up in the same manner. It was not unknown for them to humiliate their young charges by administering corporal punishment with aplomb for what we would consider today the slightest transgression. Yes, this ensured there was strict discipline in the classroom, but it left very many young boys and girls upset by their severe approach to punishment in the class.

As detailed earlier, this penalty was often administered with some force. Indeed, sometimes it could be heard through the classroom walls, with a distinctive sharp slapping noise providing evidence of an ongoing punishment. Many pupils endured the very painful penalty quite stoically and to show the rest of the class how tough they were. However, it should be noted that many boys and girls found it hard to maintain their composure during the beating. Teachers would almost certainly be charged with a criminal offence, with the possibility of a custodial sentence, if they attempted this practice today.

One of the worst examples I remember was in the GHS in 1957, when one of the teachers used the belt on every boy who did not get, in his opinion, a satisfactory grade in their exam. While it was generally accepted that corporal punishment would be administered for unruly behaviour, but to be used on pupils who, through no fault of their own, were not the cleverest in the class, was completely unacceptable. What made it worse was that the class was told before they sat the exam that this would be the punishment for failure, so it can be appreciated the pressure everyone was under to achieve pass marks. As Voltaire once almost said, "Sir, I might not agree with what you say, but I shall defend to the death your right to be a complete axxe". Many other stories of teachers who overstepped the mark in administering this form of punishment were often told at the time.

A case in point was a certain French teacher who shall remain nameless, mainly to protect me, in case he still has his belt and comes looking for me if he reads this. His skill with the belt was legendary and he could have so-called tough boys on their knees in tears if they incurred his wrath. Because of this, we always made sure our homework was completed on time and we would never, ever dream of talking out of turn in his class. A fearsome fellow was our Mr X.

It should be noted that pupils who were given the option of three blows with the belt or writing a hundred lines for a transgression, invariably accepted the former, in order to get the punishment over with as soon as possible.

Thankfully, this practice has now long ceased to exist. However, while this penalty might seem unacceptable to the present generation, it should be stressed that it did have one redeeming feature, insomuch as it ensured discipline in the classroom was, in the main, upheld.

In 1982 a judgment of the European Court of Human Rights about parental choice in education led indirectly to the use of the tawse (and all other forms of corporal punishment) being banned by law in UK state schools.

In addition to the perils of the dreaded tawse, there was also the danger of "friendly fire": when certain teachers had no hesitation in throwing pieces of chalk at pupils. In one particular case I well remember, one of them tossed a wooden chalkboard duster at a pupil who he considered was not paying attention.

A pal of mine at least managed to render one of the most disliked primary school lady teacher speechless when he continually held up his hand and said: "Miss, I need to pee". The exasperated teacher gave him a withering look and said: "May I leave the room, please?" Quick as a flash, my pal came back with "Yes, you can, but can you hurry back as I desperately need a pee?" Cannot top that.

When I was a 14-year-old, back in 1957, school was certainly not my favourite place to go to in the morning. However, every so often a lesson awakened me from my slumbers and grabbed my full attention. One such occasion was a science lesson which became part of school folklore.

It came about when the class was shown how to mix gas and air in a small coffee tin with a snap-down lid. The bottom of the tin had a small hole to let the mixture escape. The object was to light the escaping gases with a Bunsen burner and let it blow the lid off. This we did under supervision and, sure enough, off popped the lid to our universal acclaim.

Yes, we were all suitably impressed by this gas expansion experiment, but some of the class thought they could improve upon it and decided, when the coast was clear and the teacher was elsewhere, to conduct their own experiment. Out went the little coffee tin and in came a much larger dried milk tin that had a lid on the outside. To make it harder for the lid to come off, it was taped onto the body of the tin with a large portion of sticky tape. Looking back on it now, this was the experiment's Achilles' heel, without a doubt.

Next came the tricky bit: filling the tin with the gas and air mixture and lighting it. Yes, a possible disaster in the making, but the class was determined to find out how far the lid would fly off to when the gas expanded.

Breaths were held; indeed, it was so quiet that you could have heard a butterfly land on a dandelion. So, as we sucked in enough oxygen through clenched teeth that would fill a Zeppelin airship, we battened down the hatches and hoped our parents had kept up the payments on our life insurance. The temperature dropped by ten degrees, the sky darkened, and in the trees outside the birds took flight as they sensed Armageddon was about to descend on us from a great height.

An extended lit taper was gingerly held over the small exit hole at the bottom of the tin. Suddenly, instead of the lid blowing off, our mini Apollo 13 moon mission shot into the air with an explosion that would have switched off a heart pacemaker at 50 paces. In addition to almost bursting everyone's eardrums, and with a few trouser accidents along the way, it was reckoned it just about broke the sound barrier between take-off from the table and almost crashing into the ceiling of the science classroom. This was a triumph of lunacy over common sense.

Apart from the thud of dropping jaws, stunned silence reigned for about ten seconds as everyone waited for their hearts to start beating again. Then there was a mad scatter for the door before the teachers came running in to see what had happened and to find out if the classroom was still habitable. A veil will now be drawn over the painful inquest into our version of the Manhattan Project (the American research which produced a viable atomic bomb).

Understandably, this story has been somewhat embellished many times over the years when old school friends meet. However, the basic premise that there was an unauthorised experiment, and that there was a small explosion which caused many a boy to have a severe bout of micturition (discharge of urine – I'm sure most readers will guess what this signifies) is reported to be true.

You would think that, following this painful experience and the opprobrium it occasioned us from our teacher, we would refrain from experimenting with anything that made a louder noise than a sneeze or a sudden bout of flatulence.

Nevertheless, shortly after the exploding tin escapade, another lesson was given in the science class that also had our full and undivided attention.

This was in the shrine of a teacher nicknamed "Mad Andy", However, looking back now, we did him, and many other teachers, a great injustice because many of us did not appreciate how privileged we were to be taught by such dedicated teachers (well, most of them were).

As it was nearing the 5th November Guy Fawkes celebrations, our intrepid teacher thought it would be appropriate to tell us a bit about the principles of making fireworks and detailing a few of the basic constituent parts required in their production. Can you imagine that today? The teacher comes into the class and announces, "Good morning, children, today I'm going to tell you how to make a small bomb". I'm pretty sure he or she would find themselves in the Scottish equivalent of the Guantanamo Bay detention camp in the blink of an eye.

Of course, the school didn't actually make any fireworks or encourage their manufacture; it was just part of a more comprehensive lesson on combustible materials. However, when my friend Iain and I heard this, our fertile young imaginations went into overdrive and we decided to try and make our own do-it-yourself fireworks.

Considering our young age (14 years old at the time), how we managed to buy a small amount of the saltpetre and sulfur that were the main ingredients without raising any suspicions is extraordinary. In addition to the previously mentioned elements which we bought, we also needed iron filings to complete our gunpowder extravaganza.

These were easily obtained, as my engineer father had a small workshop in the Rankin Memorial Maternity Hospital where we lived, and he let Iain and I access this facility at any time.

Once we got hold of an old piece of scrap cast iron, we filed away at it for all we were worth until we had a large supply of the third element we needed to make the gunpowder (although we were told later that charcoal could have been used instead).

We then mixed what we guessed was the proper ratio of these elements together and packed them tightly into a little Smartie-type cardboard tube, with a small taper sticking out of the top that we would use as a fuse. As they say on TV, "Please don't try this at home!"

I should stress that we did not let anyone else know what we intended to do, as we were afraid word would get back to our parents and they would put an immediate stop to our foolhardy antics.

A few evenings before Bonfire Night, we took the two home-made fireworks we had nefariously produced back into the hospital grounds, which had a large clear area surrounded by trees and bushes. Cautiously, we stood the tubes upright in the ground. Next came the decisive moment as we lit the taper and ran like the wind to get behind the nearest tree for shelter.

This was undoubtedly our squeaky bum time, as we waited with buttocks clenched, and wondered if the fireworks would just go out with a little whimper, or worse still, would they explode and blow us both to smithereens and put the pregnant ladies in the adjacent maternity hospital into premature labour? A perfect summing up by writer Oscar Wilde of how we felt was when he once wrote, "The suspense is terrible, I hope it lasts".

Luckily, none of these things happened as, instead of the bang that we were expecting would register about seven on the Richter Scale, the little tubes of gunpowder flared into a very bright light that we were sure could be seen from the moon.

As this took place a few days before Guy Fawkes Night, we thought the Nobel Prize for chemistry was ours for the taking, Splitting the Atom was going to be our next project.

Looking back now, I realise how lucky we both were, and how fortunate we were to survive into our dotage without blowing ourselves to bits. However, what a great adventure it was while it lasted.

School days from a bygone era

When I wis wee, an went to school
Awe the things there were done by the rule
Fold your arms and sit up straight
An' mind nae talkin tae yer mate

Hop skip and jump, we pass oor time
The bell it goes, so we step in line
Left, right we march up the stair
"Sit nice and quiet, and chat nae mair"

Whit are we taught? Whit's the lesson?
It's Sir Walter Raleigh, at this session
He sailed the seas in a tall sailing ship
An lay in a hammock just to get a kip

Why is he famous? Whit did he dae?
He sailed fae Kirn round tae Rothesay Bay
"Answer me correctly or not at all
Go stand in the corner and face the wall"

Ma teachers face, it was like thunder
I guess I've made another blunder
My homework, jings, I forgot tae dae
I'm in the bad books, it looks that way

I'm for it noo, I'll get the strap
I'll look in my desk and get a map
Then emigrate, that's whit I'll dae
Far across the seas tae Mandalay

© **Christine Paul**

13. Christmas

Unlike today, when Christmas television adverts seem to start in the middle of September, back in the 1940s and 50s the Christmas season did not really get under way until the second week of December. And it would be approximately the same time before you would see any sign of Christmas adverts in shops and newspapers. However, when they did appear, it was a signal for us to start making our Christmas decorations. In school, we were often given assorted coloured paper strips that we rolled into circles, joining the ends to make chains which were then hung on the classroom walls.

Just as today, Christmas time was without a doubt the most exciting period of young children's lives. Mind you, on Christmas Eve we had one big advantage over today's young children, in that we could contact Santa Claus direct. How you may well ask? Well, I can still remember, as a very young boy, writing my little wish list to Santa, then giving it to my mother, who promptly sent it up the chimney. She then told me: "Santa will get that later when he comes down the chimney". Today, not even Amazon could beat that for delivery. Mind you, as we had a roaring fire going at the time, obviously unbeknown to me my little note was incinerated long before it even reached the top of the chimney.

In addition to sending the note up the chimney, tradition dictated that we hung up our stocking on the mantelpiece or on the bedpost and left out a little mince pie for Santa and a saucer of milk for his reindeers. Ah! The innocence of youth is wonderful.

Some of the most popular Christmas presents in the early 1950s were "Compendiums". I think the general idea was to keep us amused and out of our parents' hair for the rest of the festivities, or at the very best, give them a few hours of peace and quiet. This cunning scheme of theirs didn't really work, as we were always asking them to join us for one of the included games.

Each "Compendium" usually consisted of Snakes and Ladders, Ludo, draughts and tiddlywinks. I still remember trying to get those annoying little buttons into the tiddlywinks cup. Almost impossible! I was usually nearer knocking someone's eye out than getting the little disk into its beaker.

Another very popular present for boys in the 1950s was a cowboy outfit, together with a gun belt and six-shooter toy gun which fired "caps" that went off with a loud bang when the trigger was pulled (see Chapter 2 for further details).

This present regularly outsold all other young boys' gifts at Christmas.

When it came to the movie-star cowboys, the big question then was who was the most popular cowboy role model, Hopalong Cassidy or Roy Rogers aka "King of the Cowboys"? Me, I was a "Hoppy" man. To us, he was a cool dude, almost always dressed in black. This was in stark contrast with his peers, who usually wore white or light-coloured outfits. To me, Roy Rogers was just too good to be true. He was always looking for an excuse to sing a sentimental cowboy song along with his group, "The Sons of the Pioneers", who seemed to always pop up from behind a bush or tree to accompany him.

An alternative firearm was the plastic water pistol. This was the ideal toy for hot summer days when getting wet didn't really matter.

For me, Christmas would not have been complete without a little Dinky, Corgi or Matchbox car (the ones detailed below are from a later generation than the ones I was given):

Chemistry sets were another very popular present at Christmas. Amazingly, some of them contained uranium dust, sodium cyanide and other dangerous chemicals, albeit in minuscule quantities. Numerous amounts of the kits showed us how to make small explosive mixtures and how to produce puffs of smoke, as seen in magic shows. In many ways, these were potentially quite dangerous, but no one ever seemed to come to any harm. Can you imagine these products being on general sale now? I think not, as the Political Correct Brigade would have the suppliers hung, drawn and quartered immediately.

Another not-to-be-forgotten present everyone seemed to receive was a "Magic Set". This was a box of basic magic tricks, although some were so difficult to understand, that even professional magicians would have found that sawing a lady in half easier than to get them to work properly.

Meccano was, without any doubt, one of my favourite (educational) toys. It consisted of small metal strips punched with holes, plates, and gears, with nuts and bolts – components which bolted together to become whatever your imagination wanted them to be. Cars, boats and cranes were the most popular models we made. I think Meccano instilled in me the engineering

ethos that continued when I went on to become an engineer in the early part of my working career.

For boys, a train set was one of the must-have toys. "Triang or Hornby?" That was the question. Hornby Dublo manufactured the high-quality metal train sets which dominated the market until 1963, when they were bought out by their rival, Tri-ang, which made cheaper, but excellent, plastic model trains.

My first train set was a Hornby, which consisted of

a clockwork train with some wagons on a small circular track. All it ever did was to go around and around the track, but strangely enough, it kept me amused for ages (well, fifteen minutes, maximum before a bout of boredom set in).

Most families also had a few board and card games that came into their own during holiday times, especially over the Christmas period. Amongst the card games that were very popular were Happy Families, Snap, Old Maid and Patience. Board games such as Snakes and Ladders, Monopoly and Cluedo were our family's favourite board games, and are still popular today.

One of the advantages of today's modern technology is that I do not need to explain exactly how the previously mentioned games and pastimes were enjoyed. All that any interested reader needs to do is to enter the names into an Internet search engine and voilà, the answer is almost instantaneous. Wonderful.

Vintage Pastimes

Back in the days when I was young, we had our favourite toys
Dinky Cars and Cowboy Sets were loved by all the boys
Then there were Compendiums, with lots of games inside
Ludo and Chinese Checkers, some games that were supplied

Snakes and Ladders and Playing Cards were also in there too
But arguing over who won the games made such a hullabaloo
Baking powder Submarines that dived and rose again
How on earth did they do that? We never could explain

Hornby Electric Train Sets, now they were all the rage
And reading Christmas Annuals, devouring every page
John Bull Printing Kits, now what became of them?
Stamping out your notices, they were a little gem

Not forgetting Meccano Sets and the Rocking Horse
Spinning Tops that spun around with centrifugal force
Then, we got our exercise playing with our Bikes and Girds
Today the kids are found on iPads playing at "Angry Birds"

© Jim Goodall

14. Saturday cinema matinées

Back in the 1950s, it was generally accepted that children lived in a safer environment than they do now (although listening to the news on a regular basis I'm not so sure about that). In view of this, from the early age of six, I was allowed to go to the Saturday afternoon cinema matinées with my friends (no adults) to watch films that were made for our age group. Almost every week, the programme of events was just about the same, no matter which cinema matinée you went to.

First, there was the long queue of excited youngsters waiting for the doors to open, then the orderly dash into the cinema to buy our ticket. Once in, the thrill of anticipation gripped us as we waited for the curtain to go up.

A short "funny", starring Laurel and Hardy or the Bowery Boys, got us started. Then things began to get serious as the weekly serial, such as *Flash Gordon and the Clay Men* or *Zorro the masked outlaw*, came on. This was heart-stopping action all the way, right up to the time when the hero was about to meet an untimely end, then suddenly the dreaded "Watch again next week when …" flashed up on the screen. This, of course, was to encourage us to return the following Saturday. Not that we needed much encouragement.

After we had come down to earth from the excitement of the weekly serial, next on the bill was usually a cartoon featuring Donald Duck, Mickey Mouse or one of the other Disney characters. This was followed by "Next week's forthcoming attractions", which detailed all the goodies we could expect to see the following Saturday.

Finally came the main event of the day, the "feature film". This was either a comedy, from the likes of Dean Martin and Jerry Lewis or a western, where cowboys were shooting 'Redskins' all afternoon (nearly all the Indians seemed to be called Geronimo or Sitting Bull – a case of too many Chiefs and not enough Indians I think). It should be noted that this was in the days when the Indians were nearly always the villains and were referred to as "them redskin varmints", never as Native Americans. This is one of the times when the introduction of political correctness was fully justified.

Every Saturday afternoon we absorbed all the action and believed it all. Heroic fanfares for the US cavalry and menacing drums from the Indians told us that the only good Indian was a dead Indian. Now we know differently, as for the most part the cavalry was anything but heroic and the Native American Indians got a raw deal. Most of us kids even thought that this was still actually happening in the American Wild West.

We found it easy to identify who the bad guys were because they nearly always wore a black hat (with the exception of Hopalong Cassidy and Lash LaRue, who usually bucked the system by wearing black). Conversely, everyone knew who the "goodie" was because he usually wore a white hat which was very rarely, if ever, knocked off his head, no matter how hard the fist fights with the fugitives went. These outlaws were constantly BOOOOOO-ed when they were about to do their dastardly deeds, then there was a loud YEEEEHAA! when the "goodies" disposed of the desperados. Yes, what a noisy bunch we were, shouting and stamping our feet during all the action scenes and then sitting with our knees under our chins, and our sweaters pulled up to our eyes and down over our knees.

After almost three exciting hours, we left the cinema, our enjoyment fully satiated, and looking forward with anticipation to the following week's adventures.

One of the most popular cinemas we went to when we were youngsters was the Central Picture House. The Central was situated at 128 West Blackhall Street (near to Jamaica Street) and was famous for its large roaring fire located just inside the

Figure 43 The Central Picture House

door. This fire could almost singe your eyebrows at ten paces if you wandered too close to it as you queued to buy your ticket. Opened in 1916 showing silent films for 4d (1.5p), 7d (3p), 11d (4.5p), and 1/2d (6p), It finally closed its doors after its last round-up on the 5th April 1958, with a British thriller entitled "The Counterfeit Plan".

The Central was more commonly known as "The Ranch" because of its propensity for showing westerns with Roy Rogers, Hopalong Cassidy, Gene Autry, Tom Mix, Tex Ritter, Lash LaRue and the Cisco Kid, amongst others (see pictures on the following page of our silver screen heroes of the 1940s and '50s).

These were just some of our idols. And between them, they saved the Old Frontier from outlaws at least once a week.

Not only were the cowboys household names, but their horses were too. Even today, when us old codgers are reminiscing about the cowboys we watched way back in the 1950s, one of the usual questions raised is: "Okay, what was so-and-so's horse called?" And of course, that's when friendly arguments usually start and Google and other internet search engines come into their own, as the techie wizards show off their skills by looking up the answers.

Lash LaRue   Tom Mix   Roy Rogers   Hopalong Cassidy

The Cisco Kid Gene Autry The Lone Ranger   Tonto

For those of my generation who may be interested in the names of their horses (and the stars' real names), please note the following:

1. **Lash LaRue** (Alfred LaRue, 1917-1996): Black Diamond
2. **Tom Mix** (Thomas Hezikiah Mix, 1880-1940): Tony
3. **Roy Rogers** (Leonard Franklin Slye, 1911-1998): Trigger
4. **Hopalong Cassidy** (William Boyd, 1895-1972): Topper
5. **The Cisco Kid** (Duncan Renaldo, 1904-1980): Diablo
6. **Gene Autry** (Orvon Grover Autry, 1907-1998) Champion
7. **The Lone Ranger** (Clayton Moore, 1914-1999): Silver
8. **Tonto** (Jay Silverheels, 1912-1980): Scout

Other well-known film and TV cowboys of the 1940s/1950s were:

Randolph Scott, Rod Cameron, Gabby Hayes, Dale Robertson, The Range Rider, The Durango Kid, Tim Holt, Johnny Mack Brown, Tex Ritter and, of course, A List major stars like John Wayne, Gary Cooper and James Stewart.

While investigating the cowboy legends, I came across a piece of what may be considered useless, but personal, information regarding The Cisco Kid and his sidekick Pancho.

In O. Henry's (an American short story writer 1862-1910).original story, the character is a 25-year-old desperado in the Texas-Mexico border country who bears little resemblance to later interpretations of the character as a heroic Mexican caballero. An early paragraph in the book states: "He kills for enjoyment and is responsible for at least eighteen deaths. This hombre they call the Kid – Goodall is his name, isn't it?" I wonder if his first name was possibly Jim? Thank goodness this information wasn't available when I was a schoolboy, as I can imagine running around in the school playground when some smart Alec would shout at me, "Hey Cisco! Where's your pal Pancho McDonald?"

Another enjoyable outing was to the ABC Minors at the Regal Cinema, 17-19 West Blackhall Street, every Saturday morning. Although Burger King is the current occupiers at present, to our generation this building will always be associated with the ABC Minors Club, which flourished there in the 1950s and 1960s.

Figure 44 The Regal Picture House

Figure 45 The Regal Picture House

Generations of kids sang along gleefully to the ABC Minors' song, or to vociferous renditions of the theme tunes of the day. This was followed by epic dramas such as Dick Barton – Special Agent, Flash Gordon, Zorro, Laurel and Hardy, the Bowery Boys, The Three Stooges, Tarzan, and Old Mother Riley.

Another popular cinema was the King's Theatre (latterly known as the Odeon from 1956 until 1969 when it finally closed). It was situated just in front of where the old Glebe Sugarhouse is now (2013), in Grey Place. The King's was unique in Greenock having three levels of seating, the stalls, the dress circle and the upper circle (locally known as "the Gods").

Up in the stratospheric atmosphere of "the Gods", the only seating arrangements

Figure 46 The King's/Odeon Picture House

available were wooden benches which we sat on. This was because it was where the cheapest seats were (7d, if I remember correctly – approximately three pence in decimal coinage, which works out at about £0.50, using 2013s average earnings table).

The first three rows of these benches were usually cordoned off. This was for good reason, because in the past if the film being shown was boring, the kids sitting in these rows would bomb the poor unfortunates below with whatever missiles they could get their hands on. A good strong backside was also called for (the wooden benches had no backrests on them) and, as the silver screen seemed miles below us, access to the Hubble Space Telescope would have been a distinct advantage.

The La Scala, which opened in the West Station area in 1914, was also very popular with kids in those days. Although the La Scala had quite an exotic name, it was more colloquially known as La Bugs. (I'll give you three guesses why. Yes! You got it in one).

Even though I just lived about half a mile from this picture house, I never had the pleasure of ever attending the La Scala during its cinematic era.

Oddly enough I was fortunate to briefly visit the hallowed halls of the original

Figure 47 The La Scala Picture House

La Scala opera house during a business trip to Milan in 1982.

Due to the downturn of the general public going to the movies (mainly caused by the growing availability of television), the La Scala finally stopped showing films in the mid-1960s, when it was briefly converted into a bingo hall, before being demolished circa 2000 for new flats.

Other local cinemas included the Picture Palace and the BB Cinema. The Palace (pictured) was located at the corner of Robertson Street and Brougham Street. It opened on 30 December 1929, originally with seating for 1,700. This was later reduced to 1,395. The Picture Palace was

Figure 48 The Palace Picture House

sold to the Rank Organisation in September 1955 and renamed the Gaumont.

The BB Cinema, with its art deco exterior, was opened in 1914, and was rebuilt in 1935. The building still stands (2016) at the corner of West Stewart and Argyle Streets. This was reputed to be the most comfortable of all the picture houses in Greenock.

.I can't leave the subject of the Saturday matinées without

Figure 49 The B.B. Cinema

mentioning the lady usherettes who patrolled the cinema aisles with a rod of iron. They were, to us, fearsome ladies who wouldn't stand for any nonsense when we were crawling under seats trying to get to one with a better view or just making a general nuisance of ourselves.

However, looking back on it now, it was just as well they were there, as anarchy would surely have been the order of the day with hundreds of children between six and twelve years of age let loose on their own watching films. As a matter of interest, the average children's Matinee price was about 6d (2.5 pence – at today's prices [2015], £1.00).

Cheap and cheerful our Saturday afternoon Matinees may have been, but to us they were ingrained in our local psyche for a short time when we were transported to our own fantasy world.

The following is the list of 1950s films reported to have attracted the largest audiences

Top ten films of the 1950s

1	*South Pacific*	1958
2	*The Ten Commandments*	1957
3	*The Blue Lamp*	1952
4	*The Greatest Show on Earth*	1952
5	*The Bridge on the River Kwai*	1957
6	*The Great Caruso*	1951
7	*Doctor in the House*	1954
8	*Carry on Nurse*	1959
9	*High Society*	1956
10	*I'm All Right Jack*	1959

It should be noted that the evening films for adults in the 1940s and 50s had a set format that consisted of two feature films each week. The programme normally changed on Sundays and Wednesdays. Sandwiched between the Pearl and Dean adverts and the Pathé newsreel (which often showed week-old news) was a low-budget, low-quality film that was euphemistically called a B-movie. Patrons had to sit (many said endure) through this programme before watching the main feature film.

Going to the Saturday matinée Movies

Now going to the pictures was a treat on a Saturday
To see our movie heroes at the afternoon matinée
The excitement that we felt, as the lights went down
Yes, we were about to see, the film stars of renown

The Central Picture House, yes that was the name outside
But to us it was The Ranch that it was called both far and wide
Cowboys like Roy Rogers were our idols then
They'd always beat the outlaws, time and time again

Then there was the King's, where we sat up in the "Gods"
Clambering up the hundred stairs, beating all the odds
Up there were the cheap seats; it cost sixpence each I think
Plus, another thruppence to buy a nice cold drink

For us to see the film, on the screen so far away
Twenty-twenty vision was the order of the day
We'd sit and watch Tarzan, swinging through the trees
And then there were the cartoons, oh boy how we loved these

Not forgetting the Regal, with their Saturday morning shows
Where we'd all just sing along, before the curtain rose
There also was the BB Cinema, the Palace and La Scala.
Where we would spend a few hours in our own nirvana

Alas, they have all gone, I'm sorry now to say,
But memories linger on and just won't fade away
The great times that we had when I was but a boy
Of silver screen heroes, to watch was such a joy

© Jim and Rhianna Goodall

Fortunately, apart from our school activities, the early to mid-1950s was a happy and exciting period for us. We didn't feel deprived. Few families had television, which meant we played outside in our spare time. Mind you, we were quite envious of those families whose rooftops were cluttered with H & X TV aerials.

Sundays, I regret to say, were the days that many of us did not look forward too. In the morning, off we would go to church or chapel (depending on our religious beliefs), then home for dinner. The afternoons, especially if it was raining, could be very boring for numerous children, especially if we had already read *The Broons* or *Oor Wullie* in the *Sunday Post*. Some parents would not allow their kids to play outside on the Sabbath. Therefore, they had to try and amuse themselves indoors (remember that mobile phones, computers, iPads, PlayStations etc. did not exist in those far-off days).

An alternative to this restriction was to go for a Sunday afternoon walk up to the cemetery, to lay flowers on our nearest and dearest departeds' graves. We were quite often relieved when the day was over.

Thankfully we had bicycles which, for the rest of the week, basically meant freedom. We cycled everywhere and never wore a helmet, as they were very rare in those bygone days. As stated earlier, we also played football in the streets or on any spare piece of vacant ground we could find. And if we didn't get into the team, it meant we just weren't good enough and that was that. We did not go crying to our parents, complaining about our human rights. No, we just accepted that we were just not good enough and would need to try harder. Another challenge for us was climbing trees. However daunting, they were our Everest's that had to be conquered.

In the streets, we also played cricket, kick-the-can and rounders. Among the simple toys we played with were hula hoops and yo-yos. We also had our own version of hi-tech mobile phones: two cans were joined together with a piece of string. Mind you, if the string was any more than thirty feet long, we almost burst a lung shouting through them. This, of course, made them pretty much redundant as your pal, and anyone else in the near vicinity would be able to hear you clearly enough without having to use the cans.

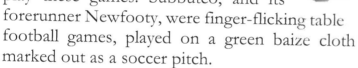

Figure 50 Our early mobile phone

A great social event we enjoyed were the Newfooty and Subbuteo leagues that were played in the winter nights. This was when we took it in turns to congregate in one another's homes to play these games. Subbuteo, and its forerunner Newfooty, were finger-flicking table football games, played on a green baize cloth marked out as a soccer pitch.

They were a physical simulation of Association Football, involving great dexterity and skill in flicking the playing figures, which stood on weighted bases, across the tabletop pitch towards the ball. Shots at goal could only be taken once the ball was over the "shooting line".

Of course, everyone had their own interpretations of the rules and many arguments took place that would put a Rangers and Celtic "rammy" to shame. Pleasant endearments such as "You're just a bawheid!" and "Away, ya numpty!" were frequently exchanged between us. As you can appreciate, these kind words were the only printable ones that can be quoted here. However, great times were had by one and all.

It should be noted that this was a "boys only" pastime. Girls to us, at that age, were a mere inconvenience. Some of the games they played were hop-scotch (the rules of which were totally alien to us), and with skipping ropes. However, as we grew older our hormones would be activated and it was then when we realised that mixing with girls could be much more exciting than playing board games.

During this period in our young lives, we even devised our "Britain's Got Talent" (or "Greenock's Got a Wee Bit of Talent") competition, long before Simon Cowell came on the scene. This was when we held our back-garden concerts and many of our friends got up to do their party pieces. That's a "yes" from me then, as Simon would say.

Every August-September time we played conkers (the seeds of the chestnut tree). First, a hole was drilled through the middle of your chosen conker, and then a string was threaded through the hole, with a knot tied at the end so that it didn't pull through. Next, we would take turns at striking our opponent's conker until one of the two conkers broke into pieces. Every time a conker broke another, it was awarded a point, and the conker with the most points was a highly prized one.

There were various ways to make your conker into a winner. The most popular method was to soak it in vinegar overnight.

However, author Roald Dahl, who was a big conker fan, suggested that "a great conker is one that has been stored in a dry place for at least a year. This makes it rock hard and therefore formidable". This may seem tame to the modern generation of children, but we had lots of fun trying to smash one another's conkers into smithereens.

Another harmless pastime we had was playing Marbles. Most young boys had bags of small glass marbles that we could add to by hitting an opponent's marbles out of a circle drawn in the street or playground. It was very important to agree on the rules before you played so that nobody could accuse you of cheating. If you wanted to "play for keeps", then you had to talk about it beforehand and agree that the winner got to keep "the hit" marbles. Playing "keepsies" was fun up to the moment when we lost our favourite marbles, which meant it was Code Red disaster.

Figure. 51 Playing Marbles

One of our preferred pastimes (after football, of course) was playing with the forerunners of go-carts we called "bogies". My pal Iain Freer and I made ours out of old pram wheels and wooden boxes, which were found in abundance in the hospital grounds where I lived.

You will note from the detail in this picture of our bogie that the latest F1 racing car's design was based on our dream machine (although, to be honest, our bogie had the aerodynamics of a brick). Once we had built the bogie, we were quite confident that we could reach a frightening five to ten miles an hour, going down a steep hill with a strong wind behind us. This prediction ranks alongside Noah on the bridge of his Ark saying that "it looks like there might be some rain today".

Figure 51 Our "Bogie"

Our bogie also had a bewildering host of gadgets that monitored our progress, such as rain, road and dynamic adjustable suspension settings, advanced traction control, parking sensors, collision warning system and a heated wooden

119

seat. Obviously, I've just made that up, but wouldn't that have been some wish list? This was another great adventure we had, one that many children in today's world would never even think about having.

Another construction exercise we enjoyed was building our makeshift "gang huts" in the garden. These huts were strictly a "boys only" domain where we met most days to put the world to rights. When I come to think of it, this practice carries on to this very day, except we meet in pubs and clubs. The only things that have really changed are the subjects of our moans and groans and the addition of alcohol. Then it was "football, films and rock 'n' roll stars". Today there is usually a medical half-hour with "what pills and potions did the doctor give you for your arthritis and old ticker this week?"

Those are some of my outdoor adventures from a different time and social clime. What lucky children we were! Do-it-yourself was so much more fun, and I suspect we were far more creative than kids sitting in front of their computers today.

Being able to make the things we wanted with our hands, and using our imaginations, gave us great confidence in our ability to produce an end product. All sorts of natural and man-made objects were grist to our mill. Is it manual creativity that's gone out of the window in the age of computers I wonder? How many youngsters today learn woodwork or metalwork at school, or knit and sew nowadays? I like to think that nothing beats the satisfaction of producing a usable handmade object. Whether it is complicated or simple, making things which actually work is, I think, a fundamental component of growing up.

Figure 52 My sons Jim & Allan with my model planes in 1977

From the age of twelve onwards, I was an enthusiastic model builder of Keil Kraft and Frog balsa wood model planes. I even continued to build these models in adulthood, as can be seen from the picture on the previous page where my sons Jim and Allan are about to launch my model stealth bombers into the wide blue yonder in 1977.

When I was seventy (in 2013), I completed my first model plane (a Spitfire – pictured here with my grandchildren Rhianna and Justin Goodall) since the mid-1970s. It was as if time had stood still when building it, as all the memories plus the smell of the wood and adhesive etc. came flooding back. Could I still remember how to put all the parts together, I wondered? As you can see, I sure could.

Figure 53 My Grandchildren Rhianna and Justin, 2013

In addition to the balsa wood aircraft I built, I also assembled plastic Airfix and Revel model planes and ships. Building them brought me so many hours of pleasure when I shut myself away in my own little world.

Figure 54 Neil St. & Sutherland Road kids outing circa 1955

Looking back, all this activity must have suited our parents, as I'm sure they were glad to get us out from under their feet and gave them some peace and quiet. The picture opposite is of some of our crowd, mainly from the Prefabs in the Neil Street and Sutherland Road area, circa 1955, on a rare day's outing. Unfortunately, I was unable to attend, as I had broken my leg playing rugby a couple of days before we went. After suffering two broken arms a few years earlier, that meant that I had managed to accumulate a hatrick of broken bones in seven years. One eminent physician diagnosed me as having a serious case of "acute clumsitisis.

16. Comics

Comic books were an indispensable method of transporting a multitude of children in the 1940s and 50s into their own little world, where imagination could transport us to wherever we wanted to be or do.

The *Beano, Dandy, Topper* and *Beezer* were the first comics I can remember reading (due to paper shortages during and just after WWII, the *Beano* and *Dandy* were printed in alternate weeks). I can even remember when Desperate Dan and company were printed in black and white.

As we grew older, we graduated to the *Hotspur, Valiant, Victor* and the wonderful *Eagle* comic, which had the intrepid spaceman Dan Dare as their front-page hero. Another great favourite was footballer Roy of the Rovers, whose exploits we read about in the *Tiger.*

As we progressed towards our early teenage years, American comics such as *Superman, Batman, Captain Marvel* and *Spiderman* were just becoming available locally. Once we had read them, we exchanged them with our friends for any of their comics we hadn't yet read.

17. Sweets and food nightmares

Once rationing ended in the early 1950s, sweets were top of our list when we were given our weekly pocket money (I remember getting the princely sum of sixpence (2.5p) a week.

When we were lucky enough to get sweets, some of the most popular ones were (note: some of them are still are available):

- **Gobstoppers** – A large, round, hard sweetie that filled most of your mouth and made talking quite a challenge.

- **Conversation lozenges** – Various-shaped sweeties with a motto or a letter on them.

  Soorplooms –Sharp-flavoured sweeties, colloquially known as "jaw clappers".

- **Toffee apples** – No wonder dentists' waiting rooms were bursting at the seams.

- **Jubbly** – A block of flavoured ice in the shape of a pyramid.

Some other favourite sweets that we enjoyed were:

The items on the previous page were our treats. However, at the opposite end of the spectrum, for me, were some of the challenging meals which were put before us on the table in those austere days. The short list below was some of my childhood food nightmares. I don't even think the celebrity chefs we have now on television could have prepared them in such a way that would have persuaded the majority of young people to eat the following gastronomic horrors:

Pigs' trotters

Nothing could strike fear into me more than the thought of pigs' trotters for tea. What's the problem with eating pigs' tootsies, you may well ask? Well, all I could think about was that they were once attached to a pig's legs, and the pig had, no doubt, been walking about in its own excrement before it had its feet chopped off at the ankles, then boiled with its toenails still intact. No amount of my mother's cajoling would make me eat them. Even today, I still shudder when thinking of them laid out on my plate.

Potted heid

This was a meat dish mixed with a gelatine solution that was made from shin bones of beef, of which the collagen forms the gelatine. It should be noted that it had a very high-fat content, which obviously did not help reduce the soaring incidence of heart disease in Scotland. This popular dish was eaten cold, with boiled potatoes. I confess I did eat it from time to time, but I doubt if I could make it pass my lips now.

Tripe

This is edible offal from the stomachs of various animals, and no amount of imagination can disguise that grisly reality. The lining of the stomach is bleached, and then partially cooked by a butcher before being sold. It then requires additional cooking at home for a further two hours before  it becomes edible (along with potatoes and onions). It is rumoured that consumption of this increases the libido fourfold. I'm sorry, but even if this was a stonewall guarantee, it's doubtful if I could be tempted to swallow this horrible delicacy.

Recently (2013), a government body, Quality Meat Scotland, planned a big sales push for tripe. This enterprise is, of course, to be applauded, as any move that encourages a less wasteful consumption of animals is welcome, but I have to say to them, "the very best of luck", as I fear they'll need it.

I personally think there should be an online Tripe and Pigs' Trotters Anonymous Society (TAPAS for short), where we could all log in and denounce this, to me, horrible food, and swear we will never let its presence darken our kitchens ever again.

Rabbit stew

No further explanation needed here. Brer Rabbit in a pot – ugghh! Recently, a friend told me he was about to partake of this delicacy, when the song "Bright Eyes", started playing on the radio. This stopped him dead in his tracks.as it was used in the soundtrack of the 1978 film *Watership Down*, featuring a small group of rabbits.

In addition to this, I also remember that the butcher's shop my mother shopped at sold "Sheep's Heid Broth", made from, yes, a sheep's head. Uggh! It should be pointed out here that chicken was considered a bit of a delicacy and was rarely available then. Indeed, I can't ever remember eating chicken when I was a young boy.

However, perhaps I am being a little bit harsh on the previously mentioned sustenance, as during extensive travels I later made in the Far East, I have had the dubious pleasure of eating shredded snake, guinea pig strips and frogs' legs, amongst other weird and not so wonderful dishes set before me.

I also just managed to avoid such delicacies as monkey brains, dog meat and scorpions on a stick by the skin of my teeth (without insulting my Chinese, Hong Kong, Taiwan, Indian and Malaysian hosts, of course), so I suppose eating pigs' trotters was possibly a much better option than swallowing their Eastern delights.

It should be noted that there were very few, if any, Chinese, Italian or Indian ethnic restaurants/takeaways in my childhood days. Only "chippies", where you could get chips, fish and chips, sausage and chips, pie and chips, black pudding and chips or, if you were flush with cash, chicken and chips along with a pickled onion.

When I was a young boy this was a period in time when every school classroom in the country had a map of the World on the wall, with the British Empire's Protectorates and Colonies marked in

Figure 55.Former British Empire Territories marked in black.

red. (Both a Protectorate and a Colony are territories of larger countries).

Amongst our heroes of the day, when I was ten years old, were Sir Edmund Hillary and Tenzing Norgay when they became the first men to conquer Mount Everest in 1953, (It should be noted that although it was a British expedition, Hilary was from New Zealand) and Donald Campbell, who broke eight world speed records on land and water in the 1950s and 1960s.

One of the most admired sports person we had then was Roger Bannister, who was the first man in the world to break the then magical four-minute mile in 1954. Bannister's record of 3 min 59.4 sec lasted just 46 days before it was beaten by John Landy of Australia. Roger Bannister had achieved this record with minimal physical activity, as he was also training as a junior doctor at the same time. The mile race is very rarely run in major competitions now, as it has been superseded by the 1,500 metres. Indeed, the current mile record of 3:43.13 (as of July 2018) has stood since 1999.

We were repeatedly told that the Sun never set on the British Empire. We were also regaled in school with stories of our great explorers: missionary David Livingstone, together with Mungo Park and Cecil Rhodes, working in darkest Africa, Captain James Cook in Australia, General James Wolfe's siege of

Quebec, Canada; John Rae who explored much of Northern Canada and found the final portion of the Northwest Passage. Captain Scott's ill-fated race to reach the South Pole, and Sir Ernest Shackleton's Antarctic expedition.

We were taught about the defenders of the British Raj in India and Baden-Powell's role in the Relief of Mafeking in South Africa. This was just a few of the "heroes" of the Empire. Yes, jingoism was rife when I was a schoolboy. Although it is perhaps a sign of these Internet times that several of the pioneers named above have had some of their achievements somewhat debunked.

Unfortunately, or as many would think, not before time, the 1950s were the period when the British Empire was starting to crumble, as many of the countries, then under British rule, fought for their independence.

Examples such as the opposition encountered in Malaya (now Malaysia) and Kenya. Our withdrawal from Palestine, Burma (now Myanmar) and Ceylon (now Sri Lanka). India had already won its independence in 1947 but then endured bloody partition from Pakistan. Eventually our Empire, together with the French, Dutch, Belgium, Italian and Portuguese Empires evaporated in varying degrees of bloodshed.

19. Coronation

Almost immediately after Hilary and Tenzing's British expedition's conquest of Mount Everest the day before the Coronation of Queen Elizabeth II on the 2nd June 1953, it was lauded as a fitting accolade to the greatest national event we youngsters had ever experienced.

The excitement that mounted every day leading up to the big event cannot be overemphasised. We even had a holiday from school and were given, if my memory serves me correctly, a tin of toffees with the Queen's portrait on the lid and a red tin Post Office bank (with no money in it). A veritable feast of goodies, indeed.

Before the Coronation took place, there was a minor concerted effort by the Scottish National Party to advocate for the Queen to be called Elizabeth I in Scotland, on the grounds that the previous Elizabeth had been an English Queen, not a British one. However, this objection faded gradually over time.

After much discussion between Buckingham Palace and the BBC, it was finally agreed that a live broadcast of the Queen's

Figure 56 Coronation of Queen Elizabeth II - 2nd June 1953

Coronation on 2 June 1953 could go ahead. This was to be the biggest outside broadcast (OB) the BBC had ever attempted.

Many streets throughout the country were deserted as more than 20 million people crowded into the homes of the minority who owned television sets. Friends from near and far appeared out of the woodwork beseeching them to let them watch the great event on their TV. It was also the biggest single boost for television sales since they had become readily available to the general public. One million new TV sets were bought or rented to watch the OB. Yes, this was the first must-watch TV programme that we had ever encountered.

As the Goodall family didn't have a television at the time, I was one of the many who sought out a pal lucky enough to have one. My pleading paid off, as my friend Scott McCaughey invited me to his prefab house in Wren Road to watch the big event on his family's TV. It should be appreciated that in the early 1950s if your family had a TV, you quickly found out that you were the most popular boy in the neighbourhood. Scott suddenly discovered that he had more friends than he realised.

I was ten years old when this, to us, was an extraordinary event we were witnessing. Apart from seeing television sets through the windows of electrical goods shops, this was the very first time I ever had the opportunity of sitting down and watching a television broadcast, and I was completely in awe of it.

On the big day, it looked as if half of Greenock had crowded into Scott's parents' living room to watch the big event. The only thing missing was the usherette with the ice cream tray and the all-probing torch. Although, to be honest, after a few hours of the solemn ceremony in Westminster Abbey, some of us boys got a bit bored and drifted outside to play football in his garden.

It is noteworthy that many of the British Establishment were not in favour of the Coronation being broadcast. They were suspicious of what they saw as, in their opinion, the vulgarity of television. Indeed, Winston Churchill, the incumbent Prime Minister at the time, was firmly against the broadcast. He is rumoured to have said, "Why should the public get a better view of it than me?" Thankfully, the persistent lobbying of the BBC by the general public and press ensured that the transmission went ahead.

20. Television

There was great excitement when, in 1954, the Goodall household eventually got a television set. Our state-of-the-art TV was a Pye 14-inch, 405-line cathode ray tube black and white set (pictured opposite). Although it had a major presence in our living room, by today's standards, it was tiny, but it dominated the room in a way its technically superior descendants never quite manage. It gave us an instant portal

Figure 57 Pye B&W 14" Television

to a cavalcade of information, variety and news. This was the era when the TV set was a weighty piece of furniture, of which the screen was only a small part. It may look very antiquated compared with the 55-inch, flat-screen, Smart 4K UHD, OLED monsters which now permeate our living rooms, but to me, it was quite literally the greatest thing that we had ever seen in our young lives.

Today we have "on-demand TV" that allows us to watch any show we want, and at any time we want it. Whereas, and I appreciate that anyone born after 1980 will find it difficult to comprehend, this was a time when things were "on the telly", and if you weren't sitting in front of the screen at the same time as the programme was being shown, you missed it completely. Therefore, the streets would fall quiet and burglary rates would nosedive when popular programmes were being broadcast.

Another consequence of having a large proportion of viewers watching a favourite programme was that when it finished, this was the time when kettles all over the country were being boiled for a cup of tea, and the national grid went into overload. Indeed, power stations had to take account of this spike in demand and act accordingly to ensure that there were no power cuts.

Unfortunately, back in the '50s, television sets were nowhere near as reliable as they are now, as it was quite common for the unhappy viewer to bang on the top of the wood-panelled sets a few times each evening to stop the picture slowly sliding up and out of the top of the screen, to reappear miraculously from the bottom of it again. If the banging didn't fix it, a call to a local TV engineer was required. He'd visit the house with his soldering iron etc., disappear behind the large wooden cabinet and replace a few capacitors, charge you a jaw-droping £10, and then be on his merry way. This was a small fortune in those days, as it almost amounted to the average working man's wage.

The nightmare scenario was if it could not be repaired *in situ* and it had to be taken away to the workshop to be fixed. This was a double whammy for the unfortunate householder because it would normally mean that the repair bill could bring strong men weeping to their knees, and even worse, the family would need to revert to staring at four walls while listening to the wireless or reading a magazine or book.

The size of the TV screen was important, indeed in many households it was considered as a status symbol. A 14-inch set was the basic size the majority of people had, but those who wanted to flaunt their wealth would splash out on one with a gigantic 17-inch screen. To avoid the expense of purchasing one of the larger-screen sets, some TV-owners bought a special

magnifying glass containing pressurised oil, which was suspended over the front of the small screen. Unfortunately, this also degraded the picture somewhat, so this innovation soon went the way of the dodo bird.

The price of our TV was circa £54, which was a very large amount of money for the average householder to pay. Today (2016) this equates to approximately £900 calculated by the Retail Price Index, or £2,300 according to average earnings. As this was way beyond the reach of the average working man's wage (£11 per week then), the vast majority of families, ours included, would rent their television set for about £1.00 a month (0.25p/week. This amount included the cost of repairing any breakdowns (these occurred quite often since TV sets were nowhere near as reliable as they are now).

As well as the rental, there was the added cost of the annual TV and radio broadcasting licence – £3 (for the one and only BBC black and white TV channel). Calculated in terms of 2012 average earnings, this would equate to about £160.

Figure 58 Combined Radio and TV Licence

In those early days of television, there was just the one BBC channel available to watch. ITV didn't start broadcasting commercial television until 1955, and this was only in London and the south-east of England. It was a few years later before the whole country could access the signal for it.

It was great when we could finally receive a second channel in the late 1950s. However, it did cause the occasional family feud when someone wanted to watch something "on the other side".

The BBC television channel in the 1950s conveyed a traditionalist English middle-class view of the world to millions of homes. This was the age of *Andy Pandy* and *Billy Bunter*, of *Fanny Cradock's* cooking lectures and *Joyce Grenfell's* monologues, *The Brains Trust* and *Noel Coward's* plays. It was also an era when interviewers showed great deference to their guests and wouldn't dream of asking intrusive questions.

Children's TV didn't start until 5.00 p.m., so we usually went out to play after school. However, the streets and play areas soon emptied just before the programme's starting time. As television sets took about five minutes to warm up before the picture appeared, we sat for what seemed a lifetime, waiting in mounting anticipation and excitement for broadcasts like *The Lone Ranger, The Adventures of Robin Hood, Ivanhoe, The Adventures of William Tell, Heidi, Champion the Wonder horse* and *Crackerjack!* to start.

When our programmes finished, the BBC closed down for the "Toddlers' Truce". This was a piece of early British television scheduling policy which required transmissions to terminate for an hour each weekday between 6 p.m. and 7 p.m., from the end of Children's TV to the start of the evening schedule. The policy behind this strategy was that young children could be put to bed before the adults' programmes commenced.

When the evening transmission started, we had to wait again until the set "warmed up",  before the picture came on. Ten minutes before the appointed time, the first thing to appear on the screen was the Test Card (pictured), which was used for calibrating and aligning the screen if need be, and it often was. Next came the BBC's heraldic crest, followed by the BBC TV newsreel with its familiar masthead encircled by spiralling airwaves.

In those early TV days, the BBC was so upper crust that announcers such as Peter Haigh, Mary Malcolm, Sylvia Peters and MacDonald Hobley. were always clad in black tie formal wear by the men and in chic gowns by the ladies and spoke in impeccable Received Pronunciation English. No regional accents were allowed to pollute the airwaves in those heady days.

Quite often in the early days of television, the evening broadcast would suddenly disappear, and we were obliged to watch one or more of the BBC's memorable "interlude" shorts, while engineers tried to resolve the breakdown problem. One of the most famous was *The Potter's Wheel*, in which a potter's hands (the potter was never shown)

Figure 59 TV Interlude (to cover service breakdowns)

would make various vase-type objects on the wheel, but never actually finishing any. These interludes usually followed a polite, card-borne "technical hitch" apology, headed with the assurance that "Normal service will be resumed as soon as possible". The strangest thing was that we didn't dare take our eyes off the screen in case the programme suddenly started and we might have missed something.

The evening broadcasts were brought to a close about 10.30 p.m. with the *Epilogue.*. This was when a clergyman would give a sacred reading and comment briefly on it. On completion of this brief Sermon, the National Anthem was played. Many a family stood up and sang along respectfully to it (not our family, I might add).

Even after we had switched off our TV sets, countless households still sat there in stony silence and watched as the tiny glowing dot in the middle of the screen slowly disappeared into oblivion. It has been claimed that the 1950s were the Golden Age of Television. Well, maybe they were. However, as with most eras, there were both good and bad times, especially since the clear majority of programmes were live broadcasts.

Nevertheless, TV was certainly fresh and new then and very much a novelty to be enjoyed.

Now, in the year 2018, as we click our way through a multitude of nondescript channels, we often find that we are either bored or apathetic about what we find there. That's when my mind often wanders back to those early days, when the excitement of watching television broadcasts, that had only one black and white transmitted BBC channel, captivated us all.

Now moving on to the mid-1950s, I was now at an age when I became more aware of the music scene infiltrating the airwaves, especially as the influence of the old guard of middle-of-the-road crooners was on the wane. The bedrooms of previous generations of teenagers were largely dismal places. (Indeed, nobody was called a "teenager" until our generation came along.) Teenage bedrooms were often testaments to boredom and tedium. What we wanted was our pop star's pictures on the wall, along with music that we could tap our feet to. So we transformed it from a soulless room into our own little nirvana.

One of the first British music genres we snapped our fingers to was called Skiffle. This was a kind of "make-do-and-mend" pastiche of American folk music, which was born out of post-war austerity. The music was performed by small groups of mainly teenagers, whose instruments usually consisted of acoustic guitars, a tea chest with a broom-handle and a piece of twine, which was a home-made substitute for a double base. In addition to this, a washing board strummed with thimbles on the fingers was often used.Most of the band members made or adapted their own instruments. The simple reason for this was so that budding young musicians could keep their costs down to an absolute minimum.

Skiffle was arguably Britain's very first homegrown pop category, and Lonnie Donegan was the most famous exponent of this type of music. Traditional (Trad) jazz was also quite popular, with the likes of Humphrey Lyttelton, Kenny Ball, Acker Bilk and Chris Barber playing music that was a revival of American Dixieland/Ragtime, updated to a mid-20th-century idiom. Trad jazz is still popular in many music circles today.

This all changed in the mid to late '50s and early '60s, with the rise of more affluent teenagers on the music scene, and when the electric guitar became king, and signalled the arrival of rock 'n' roll, with Bill Haley's "Rock Around the Clock" in 1955 This then opened the floodgates to considerable adult anxiety. Parental concern increased the following year when Elvis Presley entered the British Top 20 chart (itself a '50s invention) for the first time and put the earlier music styles on the back burner.

From that era, has there ever been a better opening line in recorded musical history than Little Richard's 1957 cry of "A-wop-bom-a-loo-mop-a-lomp-bom-bom!" in "Tutti Frutti"? Never heard it before? Put it on your Bucket List. This totally blew away all the middle-of-the-road music we had been listening to before. It was jaw-dropping excitement the first time we heard it and, for me, it's never really been bettered since.

The following were the best-selling singles of the 1950s:

	Song	*Artist*	*Year*
1	"Rock Around the Clock"	Bill Haley	1955
2	"Diana"	Paul Anka	1957
3	"Mary's Boy Child"	Harry Belafonte	1957
4	"The Harry Lime theme"	Anton Karas	1950
5	"What Do You Want to Make Those Eyes at Me For?"	Emile Ford	1959
6	"Jailhouse Rock"	Elvis Presley	1958
7	"What Do You Want?"	Adam Faith	1959
8	"Living Doll"	Cliff Richard	1959
9	"All Shook Up"	Elvis Presley	1957
10	"All I Have to Do Is Dream"	The Everly Bros.	1958

For those who may be interested, the first Number One was "Here in My Heart" by Al Martino, in November 1952. This exalted position was garnered from a pool of 52 record stores which were willing to report on their sales figures and was published by the *New Musical Express* on 14 November 1952, giving Al Martino a place in *The Guinness Book of World Records.*

As this is my book, I thought I would take this opportunity of boring you all with my Top Ten favourite songs of the period covered in this book (although I squeezed in the Glenn Miller tune from 1940, even though I wasn't born until 1943). I'm sure, after reading the list, many will think, "What a load of old rubbish!" or "Would you believe it? so-and-so! Is missing", but that's the beauty of it – everyone has their own special songs and genres which reverberate down the years.

Almost every time I look at the list, I change it slightly as I remember some long forgotten favourite that should be in the top 10. I'm sure most people would do the same.

Nevertheless, going to print, this is my list (although after printing and publishing it, I'll almost certainly remember some other song I should have included):

In chronological order:

Song	Artist	Year
"Moonlight Serenade"	Glenn Miller	1940
"Tutti Frutti"	Little Richard	1957
"Reet Petite"	Jackie Wilson	1957
"Diana"	Paul Anka	1957
"A Teenager in Love"	Marty Wilde	1959
"Will You Love Me Tomorrow?"	The Shirelles	1960
"Can't Help Falling In Love"	Elvis Presley	1961
"Runaway"	Del Shannon	1961
"Only the Lonely"	Roy Orbison	1961
"Crying In The Rain"	Everly Brothers	1961

Listening to all the songs on the radio was fine, but what I really wanted was a record player, so that I could buy my favourite 45 rpm (singles) discs, which had replaced the old 78 rpm records, especially as each person's record collection was regarded as a revealing window into their psyche, depending on your preferred music genre.

Although today's younger generation are spoilt for choice as they get their music by streaming from websites such as Spotify, Google, Microsoft, Amazon and Apple, I note that in 2017 the 12" long playing vinyl records that we used to buy, are making a comeback.

Eventually, my parents relented to my pleas for a record player, but suggested it would be better if I had a tape recorder, then I could record the songs I wanted from the radio. I wholeheartedly agreed and couldn't wait to see what they had bought for me.

A few days later, a Grundig reel-to-reel tape recorder arrived. This wonder of the

Figure 60 Grundig Tape Recorder

age cost a massive £45. It should be borne in mind that my father was earning about £15 a week at this time, so that was three weeks' wages it cost, getting me my dream machine. To this day, I still very much appreciate the sacrifice they must have made for me to have it.

I can still recall the excitement I felt when I recorded all our voices and played them back. I then connected it to the back of our radio to record my favourite songs. Today's young people would regard this as caveman technology, but back in the early 1960s when I acquired this technological marvel, it was a complete mind-blowing delight.

Continuing in the 1950s, other milestones come to mind, some trivial and some momentous. I can still remember seeing my first ballpoint pen and thought it had to be dipped into the inkwell before it could be used, then there was the arrival of packets of crisps with their little blue ubiquitous bags of salt, the wonderful LEGO, and Wagon Wheel chocolate biscuits, which seemed so much bigger in those days. Then there was the excitement when we first tasted Creamola Foam powder that was mixed with water to give us a fizzy drink - sheer bliss (the last can came off the shelves in 1998).

Two of the most memorable events that hit the international headlines, even to my young and fertile imagination, was the excitement, and conversely great concern there was around the world when Russia launched the world's first space satellite (Sputnik) in 1957. This surprising success hastened the American Sputnik crisis; and indeed, triggered the Space Race.

Another event that shocked the world was the tragic Munich air disaster of 1958, when eight Manchester United first-team players, as well as 15 journalists and passengers, were tragically killed when their plane tried to take off in a blizzard at Munich airport. These were the "you remember where you were" when you heard this news item.

Some other major events that took place during this era was the opening of the first motorway (M1) in 1959 and the discovery of DNA. Internationally, the world saw the drama of the Hungarian Revolution, the Suez Crisis, and the conflicts involving the influence of the rival superpowers of the Soviet Union and the United States culminating in the Korean War (1950–1953).

This is just a small selection of the memories that have come flooding back. Unfortunately, there are too many of them to relate here. However, I think I'll save them up for a possible "A Greenock Memoir" – part 2.

Names from the past

I remember the days when I was quite young
Names from the past would trip off the tongue
Too many to mention in this little rhyme
Are no longer here, and it's such a crime

The shipyards, sadly, have now left the river
But their glorious past remembered forever
Plus, the Glebe where my Dad toiled for many a year
And Kincaids where I worked as a marine engineer

The Ranch where the cowboys and Indians fought
And the Greenock High School, where I was taught
The Empire Theatre, where you'd get a good laugh
The Bogle and Bodega, where you'd get a cheap half

Like McAulay's the bakers, and Mazzoni's café
They are some of the many that's long gone away
But let's look to the future and what it may hold
And enjoy life to the full before we're too old.

© Jim Goodall

Blue Acre Loch Thom Smiths T C B

Prentices Shannons Crystal Palace McVeys

Strone Gails The Empire French Cross Rossini's Princes Pier

Warehouse Shannons Hotel Odeon Hector McNeil The Vennel Caddiehill Laundry

I Gordon ionaBar "The Broo" Baths Palladium

"The Bee" McNeil Templetons A McVeys

144

My thanks go to Jack Glenny for allowing me to include his wonderfully evocative poem that encapsulates his recollections from Greenock's past in its local vernacular.

Time passes so fast there's a lot left behind
That I must record before it's out of my mind
One hundred and one little thoughts of the past
Dear to my heart from the first to the last

What of the town that once used to be
What of the people who lived there with me?
I remember the smoke from the hospital lum
The Mortons' two players called Divers and Crum

The misshapen stairs in my granny's wee close
The piggery corner where you aye held your nose
The horses that struggled to climb Lynedoch Street
The Tail o' the Bank with the American Fleet

Scott's horn as it sounded at twenty to eight
The mad clatter of feet as men poured in the gate
Dunlop's buses tae Largs, Ritchie's wee ferry
Anderson shelters tae hide frae the Jerry

The man wi' the bell that sold the soordook
Fishing for trout wi' a pin for a hook
Nights in cauld winter playing "ring bang an' scoosh"
The Minister's car that aye needed a push

Enders of loaf, a big tattie scone
The "Home and Colonial", Mackenzie the pawn
A run on your bike tae the Battery baths
"Big Mick" in the school that once taught me maths

The market at High Street, Sugarhouse Lane
Princes Pier Station for the Kilmacolm train
The Mill lassies' giggles as homewards they go
Doon Drumfrochar Road past Cotton Mill Row

The Sugarhouse steam, the Oil and Cake Mill
The Dandy, The Beanoand Buffalo Bill
Tinkers wi' heather and tartan-shawled weans
The strange disappearance of the Toon's Civic Chains

Climbing gas lamps at the fit o' the street
"Big Ginger" the polis wi' kipper box feet
The jawbox, the dunny, peeversandtig
Picnics in summer by the auld Roman brig

Black and white telly and Jimmy Dow plays
The boy in yer class wi' second-hand claes
The wan-legged busker in Inverkip Street
ABC Minors, the Sunday School treat

Baggy minnows in jaur sfrae Murdieston Dam
The Co-op machine for slicing the ham
Tugs and destroyers, new ships on the stocks
James Watt, Victoria, East India docks

Tobacco, bananas, sugar and oil
"Keek Duffy", "The Wolf" and "Auld Puckle Coyle"
Brick baffle walls at the mouth of a close
Chips oot o' Cello's, coffee from Joe's

Edmiston's pies and Kennedy's breid
The night that we heard that Gandhi wiz deid
There were places and things not heard of today
Serpentine Walk and Bubbly Jock's Brae

The Vennel, the Bogle, the Baron Baillie's Hoose
National Dried Milk and free orange juice
Coppersmiths, loftsmen and riveters' mates
Holeborers, drillers, builders of grates

Chimney sweeps, leeries, all passed away
Historical trades of our Town yesterday
The man wi'wan arm they used tae call Wullie
Stood at the West Station an' sold ye the "Tele"

McIntyre's horses and Duncan Street stables
Rossini's Café wi' marble-top tables
Initials that bring memoriestae me
R.N.T.F and T double E

Clippies on buses wi' "seats up the stair"
The man that sold nylons at "five bob a pair"
Woolworths an' Markies in Hamilton Street
The corner at Burton's where the young bloods all meet

Gilchrist's and Prentice's, Bennett's, McKay's
Crawford's the place for your soup beans an' pies
This was the Greenock that I knew as a boy
Vibrant and lively, bubbling with joy
It'll never return, good things seldom do
But I'm glad that I saw it. Does the same go for you?

© Jack Glenny

While in this nostalgic poem vein, I thought I would also include a poem by a Greenock exile about some of her memories growing up in Greenock at the same time as myself.

It was written by Isobel Gray, a fellow pupil of mine at the Greenock High School. Isobel, now resident in America, read out the following poem that she wrote for a reunion we held on 2 September 1994, covering our years from 1955 to 1961 (my GHS years were from 1955 to 1958).

Who would think when growing up in Greenock far away
That I would go across the sea to America one day
Though leaving Scotland bothered me, it was such a thrill
To think of all the places I'd miss, the Port, the Strone, Gibshill

As a teenager, I would often go on sunny summer nights
To have a quiet drink or two and watch the Yankee fights
Doon the toon some Saturdays I would also go
And stand outside at Woolies to meet some folks I know

I remember on the bus one day, forgetting all my money
Explaining to the clippie, who didnae find it funny
She told me I was "at it" and not to make her laugh
I hoped to go right doon the toon, at Branchton I was aff.

Sitting in the pub one night, the Regal Bar I think,
Waiting for my pals to come to have a quiet drink
A battle started suddenly, and everyone went mad
It was punches, kicking, screaming; oh man, it sure was bad

A bouncer grabbed the two of them and threw them oot the door
They bounced along the pavement and then came back for more
The bouncer took abuse that night, the two of them could curse
He turned around and said to me "Their husbands, they are worse"

It's funny how the Greenock Fair signals the Monsoon
My father would gather all us weans and take us to Dunoon.
We'd all climb up to Canada Hill and look out from the top
Quietly praying amongst ourselves to wish the rain would stop

There's many things I miss from home and things I hold so dear
The most important things in life, the folks, the smokes, the beer
I really miss my Woodbine, I miss my single tips
But one thing I miss most of all is Aldo's fish and chips

To get the local news, the "Tele" you could read
To find out who's born, who's wed, who's deed
There's many times I'd walk along on a Sunday afternoon
And note that there is nowhere on earth like the hills above the toon

I'd walk the miles from Branchton, along The Cut I'd go
To look across the River Clyde, to mountains capped with snow
The mountains of Argyllshire, are memories that won't fade
Then I'd sit and eat my piece, the piece my mother made

I'd look o'er towards Kilcreggan, feeling nice and calm
The usual thing was on my piece, a hunnerweight of spam
Some of us went looking for a better life westwards towards the sun
Some of you have remained the same, but one thing that unites us —
Tonight we've all come hame

God Speed Greenock
© *Isobel Gray*

23. First camera

It is now 1958 and I am 15 years of age. I have just left the Greenock High School after three quite unproductive years. I should stress that this was not the school's fault. No, it was my failure to give my studies the time and dedication I should have. However, I was very lucky in quickly obtaining a job at the local marine engineering works of J.G. Kincaid & Co. Ltd. Details of my time there and subsequent career after that can be found in my little book, *Engined by J.G. Kincaid* that can be found online at www.Amazon.co.uk

This was also about the time when I became very interested in photography, a hobby I still pursue to the present day. So, as I was now earning a small wage of £2.00 per 44-hour week, I saved up my money until I had a sufficient amount to buy my first camera. When I finally had enough, and with the money burning a hole in my pocket, I duly went off to the photography department of Boots the Chemist and bought a Kodak Box Brownie, my first of many cameras, for two pounds and four shillings (£2.20), which included an eight-

Figure 61 Kodak Box Brownie (first of many cameras I had)

picture black and white spool of film. Buying the camera was the easy part. Learning how to use it was another thing altogether.

It should be appreciated that this was in the days long before digital cameras were even thought of. The Brownie camera, and many other makes like it, had to use a spool of film that captured a negative picture. Negatives are usually formed onto a transparent material, such as plastic or glass

A spool of roll film was usually loaded on one side of the camera and pulled across to an identical take up spool on the other side of the shutter as exposures are made. When the roll is fully exposed, the take up spool is removed for processing and the empty spool on which the film was originally wound is moved to the other side,  becoming the take-up spool for the next roll of film. It was critical that you didn't let any light get into the film spool as it would render it useless.

As I can sense eyes glazing over with boredom at the endless instructions just for getting a film spool into the camera, I'll stop here and move swiftly on to say that the method of taking photographs also needed a great deal of practice. This was because the camera was normally held at chest height, so you had to look down through either the portrait or the landscape viewfinder. However, I soon mastered it and from then onwards, right up to the present day, I have thoroughly enjoyed my hobby of taking photographs. My only regret is that I no longer have any of the pictures that were taken from this bygone era.

Today you can see your pictures almost immediately via your camera, mobile phone, computer or tablet. Back then, when you wanted your eight black and white pictures developed, you had to take your film spool to a chemist's shop or send it away to a specialist developing company. Then came the anxious wait of about a week before you got your precious black and white printed pictures back.

Over the years, I have had many different cameras. Today I have an outstanding camera in my smartphone and a superb Canon Digital Single Lens Reflex camera, but I can still remember, as a 15-year-old boy, the great excitement I felt as I held my very first Box Brownie all those years ago.

24. Cigarettes

Unfortunately, in my mid-teenage years, and to keep up with my peers, I started to smoke the wicked weed – cigarettes. With my newfound wealth, I now had the freedom to buy ten Woodbine (possibly one of the most iconic packets of all time) or Capstan ciggies a couple of times a week to begin with. We thought we were quite cool back then, emulating our heroes of the silver screen, not realising the health risks and financial burden we would be saddled with for many years to come.

By 1950 cigarettes were a common, everyday item with an estimated 81% of men and 39% of women smoking.

It should be noted that many respected people in the medical profession did not associate smoking with cancer back in the late '50s. I never realised then that it would take me until 1982 (when I was 39) before I had the willpower to give up the evil weed.

The estimated daily consumption of cigarettes per smoker:

Year	1949	1959	1969	1979	1990	2000	2010
Men	14.1	18.4	18.9	21.6	16.8	15.0	14.0
Women	6.8	11.0	13.7	16.6	13.9	13.0	12.0

In 1958, when I started smoking, the average price for a packet of 20 cigarettes was 3s 10d (19p).

25. Greenock Morton F.C.

Around this era (1958) some of my friends and I started going to see the "Mighty Morton" play at Cappielow on a regular basis. Now, almost sixty years later, and bearing the emotional scars of the few highs and, many would say, quite a few lows of the "'Ton" experience, I still attend some of the Saturday afternoon rituals during the football season.

For many years my friends and I stood out in all kinds of weather at the "Wee Dublin End" (WDE) before moving into the luxury of the world-famous "Cowshed" when the WDE was being converted into an all seating area. This covered enclosure, known the world over for its dedicated followers and salubrious surroundings, was our theatre of dreams. This is where we would stand on freezing cold winter afternoons, trying to stop the water dripping from our noses and wondering whether our feet were still attached to our ankles. However, the excitement of the supporters, on the occasion when there is a Morton victory, instantly blows away all our woes.

Surely there cannot be that many events which bring together people from so many diverse walks of life and religions, who meet nearly every second Saturday afternoon during the football season to cheer their heroes on. It's where you can jump for joy, sing along with total strangers, collapse in frustration and struggle to hold back tears of happiness or pain.

Most of the supporters are normal, unassuming people who wouldn't say boo to a goose. But, come the 3.00 p.m. whistle to start the game on a Saturday afternoon, a few of them mutate into screaming banshees, their banter and succinct commentary often aimed at participants guilty of playing as if they have their boots on the wrong feet.

The pithy one-liners from unconscious comedians in the "Cowshed", questioning the parentage of some poor unfortunate soul who is having a nightmare of a game, brightens up a cold and wet Saturday afternoon at Cappielow Park.

Following a particularly bad display by the team, we make our way home swearing "That's it; I've had enough, never again!" Please note that this is one of our more printable exclamations. However, come the next home game, there we all are once more, bawling our heads off at our team, urging them on to victory. That's the important thing, we have a common passion – it's our team and always will be. Yes, the Cappielow faithful are a psychiatrist's dream team. C'mon Eh 'Ton!

Figure 62 My son Jim with his nephew Justin Goodall - 2015

My pals and I had now reached the age when girls started to appear on our radar and our appearance became much more of an issue. No more was a bath or brushing our teeth a chore, it became an absolute necessity.

As our dress code was very important, being measured for our new suit at Burton's or Claude Alexander the tailors was a classic male rite of passage for our generation of teenage boys. We had reached the stage in life when we wanted to go to "the dancin'" and view "the talent". A neat suit or sports jacket and flannel trousers, along with a white shirt and "Slim Jim" tie, were the order of the day if we wanted to attract the young ladies.

The local dance halls were wonderful places in the late 1950s and early '60s. They were the palaces of pleasure where boy met girl and budding romances started. There were three popular halls I frequented on a regular basis, hoping to meet a nice girl and to be afforded the opportunity of seeing her home. Or, as it was more commonly called, "getting a lay hame". If you were lucky enough to get one, you prayed she didn't come from some outlying district miles away from your own home, as the general mode of transport then was by bus or Shanks's pony. (If you go somewhere "by Shanks's pony", you walk there.) Cars and taxis were well outwith our budget in those days.

On a Tuesday night, there was dancing at the Rankin Park Community Centre at Barr's Cottage (which was opposite the Lady Alice School in Inverkip Road, but now long gone), with Charlie Fry and the Memphis Band. Saturday evenings were also very popular when Record Hops were the order of the day. These evenings were so enjoyable that you had to queue from about 6.30 p.m. to get in at 7.30 p.m. No alcoholic beverages were sold in-house during the evening, only soft drinks along with crisps and chocolate biscuits. Come 11.00 p.m. it closed and we all left, with a young lady for company, if we were lucky.

Next came the Palladium (or the Pally D., as it was affectionately called) on a Thursday night, with its Ladies' Choice dance as a big attraction. The Palladium was situated where the Riley's Snooker Hall is now, at the corner of Robertson Street and Brougham Street.

Figure 63 The Palladium Dance Hall

I still well remember the first night some of my pals and I went there, excited, raw young teenagers, not sure what to expect. Once the music started playing, I waited and waited for about an hour, trying to build up the courage to ask some young lady for a dance, but failing dismally.

Once the first part of the evening finished, the first Ladies' Choice was called. There I stood with my throat drying up, sweating buckets, praying that some girl, oh please, any girl, would take pity on me and ask me for a dance so that I wouldn't be left standing all alone looking like a deflated idiot.

After what seemed like a lifetime, but in reality, it was perhaps only for the first few bars of Paul Anka's record of "Put Your Head on My Shoulder" played, this bouffant-haired angel appeared before me. She looked me up and down, nodded as if to say, "You'll do", then spoke the immortal word we boys all wanted to hear: "Dancin'?" The relief that I wasn't to be left standing alone at the back of the hall was immense as she took my hand and pulled me towards the

dance floor. I can't remember very much about the actual dance, or even if I ever saw her again, but I will always be grateful to her for introducing me into the Pally D.'s Thursday night rituals.

Finally, Saturday night was the highlight of the week, dancing at Gourock's Cragburn Pavilion to Henri Morrison and his Swingstars, which was the resident band. from the 1940s to the 1960s or to Charlie Harkin and his Kit Kat Orchestra, who accompanied the dancers from the 1930s till the 1990s. It was a sad day when Cragburn finally closed in 1992.

Yes, going to Cragburn was the climax of our week. Meeting up with your friends and chatting up the girls was quite stimulating. However, I suppose in many ways it was like a cattle market, with the boys standing on one side of the dancehall and the girls on the other side. Then when the band started playing, your heart beat faster as you made the dash across the floor, ready to ask the young lady of your choice for a dance. Teenagers who thought they would act cool and slowly stroll across the floor were soon brushed aside in the rush.

The nightmare scenario was if someone else beat us to our planned target. This was when we automatically reset our inbuilt GPS, in order to make an abrupt swerve and try to pounce on

CRAGBURN PAVILION

Chalmers Wood Presents

DANCING NIGHTLY

7.15 till 10.15 pm
EVERY FRIDAY
LATE DANCE TILL 11 P.M
TUESDAY and THURSDAY
OLD-TIME NIGHTS

ADMISSION:-
Monday to Thursday
Gents 2/6   Ladies 2/-   Forces 2/-
Friday   Gents 3/-   Ladies 2/6   Forces 2/6
Saturday   Gents 3/6   Ladies 3/-   Forces 3/-

AT EVERY SESSION

CHARLIE HARKIN AND HIS BAND

Resident Manager—BILL ANDERSON

some other poor unsuspecting young lady, desperately hoping to make her seem like she was our original choice.

The unobserved change of direction when crossing the dance floor was an art form in itself that many perfected with time. However, even if we were the first to reach the young lady of our choice, we were hoping and praying that we didn't have to take the long walk of shame back across the floor alone if she uttered the time-honoured rejection: "Sorry! No thanks!", or refusals to that effect.

The popular dances of the time were the quickstep, foxtrot, an occasional jive and the boys' favourite, if we were lucky, a slow blues (locally known as a "two armer"). Although my skills at dancing was average at best, the one dance I could not master was jiving to rock 'n' roll tunes. How I envied the guys who could move to this rhythm, as they were very much in demand with the girls who could also jive. However, if truth be told, some of us were quite happy sitting down and watching the girls twirling their skirts and petticoats to Elvis and his contemporaries. Like most young men of our age, the direction of our eyes was controlled by testosterone.

We had great times during this period. Drugs were almost non-existent and few people could afford to get seriously drunk. Soft drinks and crisps were about the only beverages which could be purchased inside the dance halls. Anything stronger had to be drunk prior to entry. However, intoxicated patrons were very few and far between, and any who managed to evade the doormen in their way in, were soon ejected.

Although rock 'n' roll was very popular, some of the favourites of the time were the old Glenn Miller band's swing tunes from the 1940s. The dance floor was soon bouncing once the first few notes of "In the Mood" were played (indeed, it's still almost impossible to stop tapping your feet after the first few bars).

Everything changed in the early 1960s when Chubby Checker, with his Twist and its various spin-offs, burst onto the scene. After that, dancing slowly transformed into disco nights.

Yes, going to the "Dancin'" was very popular with young people at this time. For a small entrance fee, young men and women could meet, talk and enjoy each other's company. This is where many of us met our future spouses (including me).

Although I had had a few casual girlfriends when I was 16 and 17, there were no serious romances until I danced with a certain Marion Nimmo one Saturday night at Cragburn in 1962. Marion, the same girl who had been in my class at the Lady Alice Primary School, and who had hardly ever spoken to me during the five years we were both there.

However, Marion and I hit it off right away and love was soon in the air. Following our engagement on Greenock Fair Friday 1963, we were married in the Mid Kirk, Greenock on the 7th March 1964, and spent 40 very happy years together, until she sadly passed away on the 2nd August 2004.

As this was the start of a new chapter in my life, and I was no longer a boy but a young man, it means that this little memoir has, sadly, come to an end.

When I started writing my little memoir, this was the point in my timeline where I always intended to terminate it at, as it covered the part of my life up to my early twenties when I got married, and when Marion and I had our two sons. The reason for the jottings you've just read was, therefore, to let them and my grandchildren and friends know what life was like for me and my peers from my early formative years until I got married at twenty-one years of age.

As I stated at the beginning of the book, I was born in 1943. This was when World War II was still in progress. Winston Churchill was the Prime Minister and there was food rationing throughout the land. Yet, within a dozen years, we were the first generation to grow up with television, pop music, the hydrogen bomb and the National Health Service. As a child, I even knew some men who had fought in the First World War, and many other men who did likewise in WWII. Indeed, uncles of mine were sadly killed in both these wars.

The early 1940s through to the early 1960s, the period that this book covers, was an era when we saw more changes in our lives than our forefathers had ever seen, and I was so glad to be a part of it.

Today, many children have seen more of the world than celebrated explorers like Christopher Columbus, Vasco da Gama, David Livingstone, Captain James Cook, Sir Ernest Shackleton and many other intrepid pioneers ever did.

As I have now reached what is euphemistically called the twilight years of my life, I thought I should make a 'Bucket List' of things I would like to do before it's too late. Included in my list is going to see the Grand Canyon and Monument Valley in America, the Taj Mahal in Agra, India, and the Coliseum in Rome.

However. I can't complain, as I've been very fortunate to have visited the Acropolis in Athens, the Egyptian Pyramids and the Great Wall of China (the previous two in the same week, but that's another story). I have also been to the current (2017) three tallest buildings in the world, starting with Kuala Lumpur (the Petronas Twin Towers), then Taiwan (Taipei 101) and finally Dubai (the Burj Khalifa).

I have sailed up Norwegian fjords and been to the top of their Olympic Ski Jump. In addition to this, I've been to Romeo and Juliet's (supposed) balcony in Verona, stepped inside the La Scala opera house in Milan, trodden the ruins of Pompeii and gazed upon Mount Vesuvius, best known for its eruption in AD 79 which buried and destroyed the Roman cities of Pompeii and Herculaneum.

I have been caught in a 110-mph typhoon in Hong Kong, walked through the Gateway to India in Mumbai. Strolled through Tiananmen Square and the Forbidden City in Beijing and wondered at the architectural landmarks lining the Bund in Shanghai.

I have even wined and dined with the British Ambassador at an Embassy Garden Party in Athens. Another highlight of my travels was in Jerusalem when Marion and I visited the Church of the Holy Sepulcher (the site where Jesus of Nazareth was crucified), the Garden of Gethsemane (at the foot of the Mount of Olives) and we gazed at the Wailing Wall and Temple Mount in the Old City.

In Bethlehem, we walked through Manger Square and the Church of the Nativity (This holy site is thought to be the area in which Jesus of Nazareth was born).

I have been on a six-month work secondment in Singapore, and my many other work commitments abroad have taken me to Malaysia, Hong Kong, Taiwan, China, Portuguese Macau, Dubai, Abu Dhabi, Cyprus, Greece, Italy, the Netherlands, Norway, Sweden, Denmark, Germany, Qatar, India and Kuwait. I have also set foot in Sri Lanka and Thailand. Therefore I, who was born during a war-ravaged Europe and

Japan in the 1940s, have seen more of the world than my ancestors could ever have imagined existed.

Even though I have visited all the above countries, an online survey calculated that this only accounts for about 8 per cent of the world I have been too. Therefore, I still have another 92 per cent left to see. At this rate, I will need to live until I'm about 105 before I even reach double figures. However, before going to any new destination, I always keep in mind some sound advice I once read that said: "you should think twice before going to a country where people still point at planes in the sky". How true this is when you think about it.

Today I am the very proud father of my two sons Jim Goodall and Allan Goodall, and grandfather to Nicole Wylie, Jack Wylie, Rhianna Goodall and Justin Goodall. I would like to take this opportunity to say to them, remember what you have now and what is happening around you, because when you're my age (seventy-five at the last count), the young generation will have an outlook very different from yours. They will have diverse aspirations and their lifestyle and the way of life you have now will be poles apart. You may, therefore, want to do what I have done and inform them how you live now. I am sure your descendants would be very interested in hearing how you lived way back in 2018.

Just remember, when you're young, you think you are immortal, and you think anyone over 40 is old. Then before you know it, you get to the time when people your own age shuffle of this mortal coil. So, pass on your memories to any who'll listen, before it's too late.

When I mentioned to my granddaughter Rhianna Goodall that I was writing this short story of my early life, she said that I should carry on and bring it up to the present day, and to remember that she wanted to play a part in it. So, *A Greenock Memoir, Part Two* may follow one day, especially as friends and relatives read this one and reminded me of more events that took place which I had forgotten about.

Sandwiched between the Second World War and the Swinging Sixties, which this book covers, was a period of relative calm. However, it was also a time of exhilarating new developments in technology, entertainment, music and fashion, which would prepare us, the 1940s generation of children, for the revolutionary changes we were about to experience.

Therefore, I hope dear reader, that after spending some hours you will never see again reading my little book, that you have enjoyed my, at times light-hearted little stories from a disappearing world, and that they struck a chord with some of you. More importantly, that you found that they were informative, poignant, amusing, but above all, I hope, NOT boring.

My Twilight Days

My life is at the stage now when each day is a bonus
Now these limbs of mine have an awful creeping slowness
How I wish I could run and play as I did so long ago
Oh, for another chance at it, but now I'm just too slow

So, as the day is almost over, and it's now time to have a beer
To sit and put my feet up, while my thoughts are fresh and clear
I'll close my eyes and think about the days that have now gone by
And dream of all the happy times when blue was in the sky

But now, it's pills and potions that I have to take each day
To keep the common cold and heart attacks at bay
Still, I've had a terrific life, one that's been full of joy
Great family and friends I've had; I've been a lucky boy

I often wonder what my future holds in the coming years
Like the Starship Enterprise, I'll look for new frontiers
I'll boldly face new challenges, yes that's what I must do
Embracing the world before me, along with visions anew

I'm not a Peter Pan pensioner, who dreams about the past
I have to remember here and now, that the clock is ticking fast
So, with the time that's coming, I'll try out many a new thing
And hopefully, I can see them through, before hearing Angels sing

© Jim Goodall

When You Are Old – *W.B. Yeats*

When you are old and grey and full of sleep
And nodding by the fire, take down this book
And slowly read, and dream of the soft look
Your eyes had once, and of their shadows deep

Other books by Jim Goodall:

- *Family Life 1895-1969*
  A short biographical history of my family life

- *When I Was a Working Man: 1958-2010*
  A snapshot of working life in marine engineering in Greenock, Wallsend and Singapore.

- *Engined by J.G Kincaid 1958-2000*
  Memories of my 42-year career in marine engineering, starting as an office boy on 5 May 1958 and ending on 5 January 2000 as Sales and Contracts Manager.

Contributions to other books:

- *Barr's Cottage Muses*
  A book of short stories and poems by the Barr's Cottage Writers' Group.
  Published 2014.

- *Barr's Cottage Reflections*
  Another book of short stories and poems by the Barr's Cottage Writers' Group.
  Published 2016.

- *Ironfighters, Outfitters and Bowler Hatters*
  A comprehensive recollection of the final Indian summer of volume shipbuilding on the Clyde through the 1950s to the early 1960s, by George C. O'Hara.
  Published: Clyard Novella Ltd, 1997.

This book, detailing my early life and times in Greenock, is dedicated to my late wife Marion, who I think about every day, and miss so very much.

Printed in Great Britain
by Amazon